JOBS

IN

AMERICA

JOBS

IN

AMERICA

I.G. GARVARDINA
Editor

Nova Science Publishers, Inc.
New York

Art Director: Maria Ester Hawrys
Assistant Director: Elenor Kallberg
Graphics: Denise Dieterich, Kerri Pfister,
            Erika Cassutti and Barbara Minerd
Manuscript Coordinator: Gloria H. Piza
Book Production: Tammy Sauter, Gavin Aghamore
Circulation: Irene Kwartiroff and Annette Hellinger

*Library of Congress Cataloging–in–Publication Data
available upon request*

ISBN 1-56072-372-6

© *1996 Nova Science Publishers, Inc.*
  6080 Jericho Turnpike, Suite 207
  Commack, New York 11725
  Tele. 516-499-3103 Fax 516-499-3146
  E Mail Novasci1@aol.com

Printed in the United States of America

– CONTENTS –

Introduction

The newspapers are full of articles about the downsizing of America. Workers lose more and more jobs and Wall Street cheers louder and louder. The theory is that the company being downsized will be leaner and leaner and return more and more profits to the pockets of the investors. What about the workers being downsized? Who cares! This is capitalism with a capital C folks. Some of them can take jobs in the fast food industry or cleaning services. It is not our concern says industry and government.

Except it turns our that there are some job training programs out there and even programs to retrain people. Naturally, they are very weak and not very well known. If America is to avoid a domestic and extremely volatile apartheid, somebody better take care of job training and retraining and be sure that these jobs enable the retrained people to earn an acceptable standard of living.The alternative is a high potential for civil violence and a society which will be unable to compete as the century proceeds.This modest book brings together some very interesting programs and highlights several interesting trends.

One hopes that industry and governments at every level will somehow see past their own perks and invest more and more in training and retraining programs for the poor slobs out there who appear to them to be inconvenient thorns but who can in reality be the flowers of the land if only they can get a few drops of water.

I.G. Garvardina
June 26, 1996

Training for Dislocated Workers: Which Workers? What Services?

Ann M. Lordeman

Summary

Policy makers are increasingly concerned about the plight of the approximately one to two million workers dislocated each year. Several large companies have restructured their workforces to be more competitive resulting in large-scale layoffs. At the same time, public policies in the areas of defense, trade, and environmental protection might result in further worker dislocation. Hearings on dislocated workers have already begun in the 103d Congress and the Administration plans to propose legislation to create a comprehensive dislocated worker program.

As the 103d Congress addresses the training needs of dislocated workers, it will most likely look to existing dislocated worker programs as potential models for new or revised programs. The employment and training programs specifically for dislocated workers are those authorized under the job Training Partnership Act and the Trade Act. In examining the adequacy of existing programs, Congress may address the questions of "who should receive training?" and "what training and training-related services should be provided?" The answers to these questions will, at least in part, determine the scope and cost of any new or revised programs.

Training and related services might be provided to all dislocated workers regardless of the cause of dislocation or only to workers who lose their jobs as a result of specific changes in public policy. In addition, training and related services could be provided primarily or only to dislocated workers who face the greatest obstacles to reemployment, e.g., the "hard to serve." These workers could be a subgroup for ether all dislocated workers or a subgroup of dislocated workers affected by public policies.

Any mix of the following services could be provided to dislocated workers: job search assistance; training, including basic skills training, occupational skillstraining, and on-the-job training; and income support. The services provided and the relative emphasis placed on each could be determined solely or in art by localities, States, the U.S. Department of Labor, or Congress.

In large part, the scope of a dislocated worker program will be determined by the characteristics of the workers to be served and the services to be provided. A dislocated worker program can be defined comprehensively with broad eligibility criteria and a full range of services or it can be defined more narrowly with eligibility targeted to "hard to serve" workers an with a limited number of services provided. One issue for policy makers to consider is the relationship between the comprehensives of a program and its cost-effectiveness.

INTRODUCTION

Policy makers are increasingly concerned about the plight of dislocated workers. Several large companies have restructured their workforces to be more competitive resulting in large-scale layoffs. At the same time, public policies in the areas of defense, trade, and environmental protection might result in further worker dislocation. Hearings on training for dislocated workers have already begun in the 103d Congress and the Administration plans to propose legislation to create a comprehensive employment and training program for dislocated workers.

Each year between one and two million workers, many of whom have an established work history, lose their jobs as a result of structural changes affecting the economy, and are to likely to find new jobs in their former industries or occupations. One of the major obstacles they face to reemployment is that their job skills may not match the skills required for jobs in expanding industries.[1] Congress has responded to this skills mismatch by creating training programs for them.

As the 103d Congress addresses the training needs of dislocated workers, it will most likely look to existing programs as potential models for new or revised dislocated worker programs. The focus of this report is on the issues and options to be addressed in either developing new programs or revising current programs to provide training to dislocated workers. Specifically, this paper will consider two questions: Who should receive training? What training and training-related services should be provided?

The current programs which could be revised or eliminated are authorized by two Federal statutes: The Job Training Partnership Act (JTPA) and the Trade Act of 1962. These programs provide training and support services, including income support. Title III of JTPA authorizes four programs:

- a generic program for dislocated workers regardless of the cause of dislocation.[2] This program, first authorized in 1982, is funded at $516.6 million for FY 1993.

- the defense conversion adjustment (DCA) program for workers dislocated as a result of cuts in defense spending or base closures. This program, authorized in 1990, was funded at $150 million in FY 1991. Funds are available for obligation through September 1997.

- the clean air employment transition assistance program (CAETA), for workers dislocated as a result of compliance with the Clean Air Act. This program, authorized in 1990, is funded at $50 million for FY 1993.

---

[1] For comprehensive information on the magnitude of dislocation, the characteristics of dislocated workers and their reemployment experiences, see U.S. Library of Congress. Congressiional Research Service. *Dislocated Workers: Characteristics and Experiences, 1979-1992*. CRS Report for Congress No. 91-813 E, by Linda Levine. Washington, Nov. 16, 1992. (Hereater cited as *Dislocated Workers*) Also see, U.S. Congressional Budget Office. *Displaced Workers: Trends in the 1980s and Implications for the Future*. Washington, Feb. 1993.

[2] This generic program is frequently referred to as EDWAA, the acronym for the Economic Dislocation and Worker Adjustment Act which amended title III of JTPA in 1988.

- the defense diversification program for certain members of the armed forces, certain defense employees, and certain defense contractor employees adversely affected by cuts in defense spending. This program, authorized in 1992, is funded at $75 million in FY 1993. Funds are available for obligation through September 30, 1994.

The Trade Act of 1962, as amended, authorizes a fifth program

- the trade adjustment assistance (TAA) program, for workers who lose their jobs as a result of competition from imported goods pursuant to Federal trade policies. This program is funded at $211 million for FY 1993.

This report does not describe these existing programs in great detail. For background information and a general description of the JTPA dislocated worker programs, readers are referred to U.S. Library of Congress. Congressional Research Service *Training for Dislocated Workers Under the Job Training Partnership Act*. CRS Report for Congress No. 92-901 EPW, by Ann Lordeman. Washington, December 3, 1992. For information on the TAA program, readers are referred to U.S. Library of Congress. Congressional Research Service. *Trade Adjustment Assistance: The Program for Workers*. CRS Report for Congress No.92-73 EPW, by James R. Storey. Washington, December 26, 1991.

WHICH WORKERS?

OPTION

Training and related services could be provided to all dislocated workers regardless of the cause of dislocation or only to workers who lose their jobs as a result of specific changes in public policy. In addition, training and related services could be provided primarily or only to dislocated workers who face the greatest obstacles to reemployment, e.g., the "hard top serve". These workers could be a subgroup of either all dislocated workers or a subgroup of dislocated workers affected by public policies.

> **WHICH WORKERS?**
>
> Should all dislocated workers be eligible regardless of the cause of dislocation?
> Should only workers who lose their jobs as a result of specific changes in public policy be eligible?
> Should worker who are "hard to serve' be primarily or only eligible?

CURRENT PROGRAMS

The eligibility criteria for TAA and the three smaller JTPA programs are directly related to the specific cause of dislocation. In contrast, the eligibility criteria for the generic JTPA dislocated worker program are broad. These latter criteria include workers who have been laid off from their jobs, are eligible to receive or have exhausted unemployment compensation, and are unlikely to return to their previous industry or occupation; workers who have lost their jobs as a result of permanent plant closing; workers who are long-term unemployed with limited opportunities for employment in the same or similar occupation where they reside; persons who were self-employed as a result of general economic conditions or natural disasters; and (in some cases) displaced homemakers.

None of these five programs for dislocated workers have any requirements for targeting "hard to serve" dislocated workers for services. This is in contrast to JTPA's training programs for disadvantaged adults and youth, where beginning July 1, 1993, at least 65 percent of the participants must have at least one barrier to employment, such as having a basic skills deficiency, being a school dropout, a welfare recipient, or a criminal offender. In other words, services will be targeted within the economically disadvantaged population, recognizing that not all low-income individuals are equally disadvantaged in the labor market.

ISSUES

A rationale for providing services to all workers regardless of the cause of dislocation is that the effects of dislocation ion individual workers, such as a decrease in income or loss in health insurance benefits, are the same whiter workers lose their jobs as a result of changes in consumer demand or as a result of cutbacks in defense. Consequently, some observers assert that the Federal response should also be the same.

A further rationale for providing serves to all dislocated workers, is the difficulty in determining whether a public policy is actually the direct cause of a dislocation. Many observers also assert that it is unfair to ignore the indirect effects that public policy changes frequently have on other workers. For example, it is possible to argue that cuts in defense spending affect not only defense contractors, but also suppliers to defense contractors. the defense diversification program includes defense subcontractors who had received at least $500,000 in contracts over a period of time, because some observers asserted that under the previously created defense conversion assistance program, defense subcontractors were not helped even though they were just as affected by the cuts in defense spending as were defense contractors. In some cases, it has been argued that since a whole community can be affected, workers at dry cleaners and food stores, for example, could lose their jobs and therefore should be eligible to receive services as well.

A final rationale for providing services to all dislocated workers is that a generic program can potentially promote a more comprehensive and coordinated approach to delivering services, while separate programs may increase the potential for duplication and fragmentation of services. Each separate program may have its own eligibility criteria, allowable services, and delivery system. Workers may be eligible for more than one program. For example, workers under TAA may also receive services under JTPA's title III programs. Multiple training programs for dislocated workers might be confusing to workers trying to obtain assistance. The administrative costs of operating and managing multiple programs might also be an inefficient use of scarce resources.

A rationale for providing training and related services to workers who lose their jobs a s result of a specific change in public policy is that the public as a whole is likely to benefit form the policy change and therefore those who are directly hurt by the change should be compensated. I times of scarce resources, creating a specific program for workers affected by a public policy will help to ensure that the group affected by the policy receives at least some assistance in becoming reemployed.

One reason for creating the three JTPA programs for specific groups of dislocated workers was the concern that without separate programs, these workers would have to compete with all dislocated workers for services, and might not receive assistance. Unlike the TAA program, none of the JTPA dislocated worker programs are entitlements; the number of persons who can receive services depends on the annual appropriations.

If there wee funds for all dislocated workers, training and related services provided by a generic program, there would be less reason to create separate programs.

A rationale for targeting services to workers who have the most difficulty obtaining employment is that these workers may not find employment without assistance. In general, dislocated workers with certain characteristics, such as older workers, minorities, those with long job tenure, and persons with limited education are more likely to experience difficulty in finding jobs.[3]

One project which attempted to identify dislocated workers most likely to experience difficulty in obtaining employment was the New Jersey Unemployment Insurance Reemployment Demonstration Project, conducted from July 1986 through September 1987 by Mathematica Policy Research, Inc. To be eligible for the project, Unemployment Insurance (UI) claimants had to meet the following criteria: (1) received their first full UI payment within 5 weeks after the initial claim; (2) be at least 25 years of age; (3) worked for the last employer for 3 years prior to applying for UI benefits and not have worked full-time for any other employer during the 3-year period; (4) did not expect to be recalled and did not have a specific recall notice; and (5) were not hired through a union hall.

The study found that these criteria did identify a population whose characteristics are generally associated with dislocated workers and with difficulties in being reemployed. Specifically, the study found that compared to a group of UI claimants not eligible for the project, "A substantial proportion of the eligible population were older, a substantial proportion (about 40 percent) indicated that their plant had closed or moved or their shift had been eliminated." IN addition, the study found that the eligible population compared to the noneligible population experienced, on average, considerably longer periods of UI collection and longer unemployment spells.[4]

Targeting services to the hard to serve may help to ensure that workers who need assistance obtaining employment receive it. However, it is impossible to develop targeting criteria that , in all cases, exclude persons who may not need services and include persons who do need them. Again, in the case of the New Jersey Project, Mathematica found that some individuals who were targeted for the project had characteristics similar to some who were screened out.[5] Consequently, some workers who may not have needed services, (e.g., those in the prime of their working lives and those in growing industries) may have been eligible for the project, while some workers who may have benefited from services, (e.g., those who exhausted their UI benefits) may have been ineligible.

---

[3] *Dislocated Workers*, p.22

[4] U.S. Department of Labor. Employment and Training Administration. *The New Jersey Unemployment Insurance Reemployment Demonstration Project*. Unemployment Insurance Occasional Paper 89-3. Washington, 1989. p. 47-67. Report prepared by Walter Corson, Shari Dunstan, Pual Decker, and Anne Gordon. Mathematica Policy Research, Inc., Princeton, New Jersey. (Hereafter cited as *New Jersey UI Project*.)

[5] *New Jersey UI Project*, p. 67.

WHAT SERVICES?

OPTIONS

Experts generally agree that successful dislocated worker training programs provide a variety of serves to participants. The major components of a job training program may include some mix of the following serves: job search assistance (JSA); training, including basic skills training, occupational skills training, and on-the-job training (OJT); and income support to persons while they participate in training.

> **WHAT SERVICES?**
>
> Job Search Assistance (JSA)
>
> Training
>
> > Basic Skills Training
> > Occupational Skills Training
> > On-the-Job Training (OTJ)
>
> Income Support

Job search assistance usually refers to activities designed to assist a person in finding a job. Examples of these activities are developing a resume, practicing interviews, and identifying and contacting potential employers. JSA is often provided through workshops, which can vary in length from one to several days. JSA is generally considered the most appropriate service for workers who already have marketable skills and do not require training.

Training generally consists of either classroom training or on-the-job (OJT) training. Classroom training can be either training in basic skills such as reading, math or English as a second language, or it may be skills training for a particular occupation. Basic skills training may be the only training an individual needs to obtain employment or it may precede occupational skills training. In OJT, participants receive training from an employer while receiving a wage. The employer is reimbursed by the program for a portion of the employee's wages for a specified period of time.

The purpose of JSA and training is to provide individuals with the skills they need to obtain employment. Other services, such as skills assessment, job counseling, and support services, (e.g., transportation and child care), job search and relocation allowances, and income assistance are intended to provide support to individuals while they receive training or conduct their job search. Of these services, only income support is discussed in this report, because it is generally considered the most important service in determining whiter individuals will participate in a training program.

The services to be provided to dislocated workers and the relative emphasis placed on each service could be determined by localities, States, the U.S. Department of Labor, or Congress. One option would be to leave decisions about appropriate service mix to localities based on their assessment of need. In contrast, Congress could stipulate the services to be provided and the percent of funds that could be spent on each service.

JOB SEARCH AND TRAINING

CURRENT PROGRAMS

Under JTPA's dislocated worker programs, job search assistance is one of the services that may be provided to eligible individuals. Under TAA, JSA is not specifically provided although TAA participants may receive job search assistance from the State Employment Service or from JTPA programs.

Under JTPA's dislocated worker programs and under TAA, a wide range of training services may be provided including occupational skills training, on-job-training, and basic and remedial education, among others. Under JTPA's generic dislocated workers program, substate areas operating the program generally must spend at least 50 percent of their funds on these services.[6] Under TAA, participants must be enrolled in a job training program in order to receive income support, referred to as a trade readjustment allowance (TRA). (In some circumstances, the training requirement can be waived).

ISSUES

A rationale for placing relatively more emphasis on job search assistance than on training is that JSA costs less than training, and is generally considered to be cost-effective. More persons can be served because of the lower cost per person. On the other hand, too much emphasis on JSA could result in "creaming", i.e., serving those individuals who have the least difficulty in finding reemployment because they have marketable skills.

A rationale for placing relative more emphasis on training than on JSA is that training may be necessary for those dislocated workers who need either basic skills or occupational skills in order to obtain reemployment. For these workers, JSA alone may either result in continued employment or employment in low-wage jobs. In addition, emphasizing training over JSA may result in better jobs in the long run, i.e., those paying higher wages and health benefits.

In 1998, when Congress completely revamped the STPA title iii program, there was concern that the program placed too much emphasis in JSA and not enough emphasis on training. Congress addressed this criticism by requiring that substate areas spend at least 50 percent of their funds on training. However, some observers assert that a requirement to spend a minimum amount on training can result in training being provided to individuals who may not need it. Substate areas might fund high-cost training to meet the requirement, rather than to meet the actual needs of the dislocated workers.

The difficulty in determining the relative amount of emphasis that should be placed on JSA and training is that few studies have been conducted to evaluate the effectiveness of either service. One researcher has evaluated the results of studies of the effectiveness of four major dislocated worker training demonstration projects funded by the U.S. Department of Labor in 1980s.[7] He found that JSA services have the intended effect on labor market outcomes, including earnings, placement, an employment rates, and amount of UI benefits. He concluded that given the relatively low cost per worker of JSA, it is cost effective service.

He also found that classroom training did not have a sizable incremental effect on earnings, employment, and UI benefits above that of only job search assistance. He concluded that the additional effect of classroom training is not large enough to compensate for the higher cost. Regarding on-the-job training, only one project had enough participants place din OJT slots to provide reasonably reliable estimates of the net impact of OJT programs. In that project, OJT did not consistently have a positive effect on earnings for trainees or on employment rates.

---

[6] There is no similar requirement under JTPA's three programs for specific groups of dislocated workers.

[7] Leigh, Duane E. *Does Training Work fo rDisplaced Workers? A Survey of Existing Evidence*. W.E. Upjohn Institute for Employment Research, Kalamazoo, Michigan, 1990. p. 17-50. (Hereafter cited as *Does Training Work for Dislocated Workers?*)

The evaluators of the four demonstration projects offered a number of possible reasons for their findings that classroom training was not as effective as JSA. These included "the difficulty of drawing reliable inferences from small sample sizes, the problem that program participants undergoing skill training have little time to receive placement assistance (given demonstration periods of fixed length), the scarcity of training provides capable of putting together high-quality, short-duration trainman courses on short notice, and the possibility that the classroom training provided is either not saleable in the local labor market or not of particular interest to the client population."[8] These problems may indicate the need for further research in this area.

The most recent source of information on the effectiveness of training for dislocated workers is an evaluation of TAA conducted by Mathematica Policy Research, Inc. for the U.S. Department of Labor. This study analyzed survey data from a sample of TAA trainees, Trade Readjustment Assistance (TRA) recipients and a comparison sample of UI claimants from manufacturing industries who exhausted their UI benefits but did not receive either TRA benefits or TAA training. The evaluation team found that training did not have a significant impact on employment and earnings of the trainees, at least in the first three years of the initial claim.[9]

INCOME SUPPORT

CURRENT PROGRAMS

Under the JTPA's dislocated workers' programs, income support may be given to workers who need cash assistance to participate in training if they meet certain requirements, such as being enrolled in training at a certain point in time and not qualifying for or exhausting UI. Under the generic program, the income standards for receiving these needs-related payments and other supportive services, such as child care, and transportation assistance. The requirements relating to income support under JTPA's three programs for specific groups of dislocated workers are somewhat different, but in all cases the payments are needs-related.

Under TAA, income support (TRA) is not related to need. TRA benefits are provided to eligible workers who have exhausted their UI benefits and are enrolled in a job training program. (In some circumstances, the training requirement can be waived.) TRA benefits are an extension of UI benefits. The TRA weekly benefit amount is the same as the UI amount.[10] Eligible workers are entitled to receive TRA payments for a combined maximum of 52 weeks of UI and TRA benefits. An additional 26 weeks of cash benefits can be received if the worker is participating in approved training.

ISSUES

A rationale for providing income support to dislocated workers is that some may need it in order to participate in training. For others, income support may allow them to take

---

[8] *Does Training Work for Displaced Workers?*, p.48

[9] U.S. Congress. House. Commitee on Education an Labor. Subcommittee on Labor-Management Relations. *Statement on Existing Programs to Help Displaced Workers.* Walter Corson, Mathematica Policy Research, Apr. 20, 1993.

[10] Each Stae sets the maximum limit on the UI it will pay, and this maximum applies to TAA as well. The maximums vary widely among States, even though TAA is funded as a Federal entitlement.

sufficient time to find the job that best matches their skills and experiences. However, some allege that linking income support to training encourages workers to obtain training only to receive income support and that it may actually be a disincentive for finding a job.[11]

One source of information on the relationship of income support to training is a General Accounting office (GAO) study comparing the JTPA generic dislocated worker program and TAA in three States: Michigan, New Jersey, and Texas.[12] GAO found that in each of the States, TAA workers were more likely to enroll in training lasting 26 weeks or more.[13] As stated earlier, JTPA participants are unlikely to receive income assistance while TAA participants generally receive income support through TRAs. Since GAO was not able to compare the outcomes of TAA to the outcomes of the JTPA generic program, it is not possible to say whiter the longer-term training provided under TAA is more effective than the shorter-term training provided under JTPA.

POLICY IMPLICATIONS

The options chosen to address the questions of "Who should receive services" and "What serves should be provided" will, at least in part, determine the scope and cost of a dislocated worker program. The most comprehensive and most expensive program would (1) have general eligibility criteria, (e.g., all dislocated workers regardless of the cause of dislocation), and (2) provide a full range of services including long-term training and income assistance. Conversely, the least comprehensive and least expensive program would (1) have limited eligibility criteria, (e.g., workers who lost their jobs as a result of specific changes in public policy), and (2) primarily provide job search assistance and short-term training.

---

[11] For example, numerous studies have been done which show that UI increases th etime people stay unemployed. For a review of the literature in this area, see Atkinson, Anthony Bl, and John Mickelwright. *Unemployment Compensation and Labor Market Transitions: A Critical Review.*IN Journal of Ecomomic Literature, v. XXIX, Dec. 1991. p. 1679-1727.

[12] According to GAO, these States accounted for aobut 31 percent of TAA participants and 24 percent of TAA expenditures during FY 1990. They also represented about 14 percent of EDWAA participants and 19 percent of EDWAA expenditutes during PY 1990. See: U.S. General Acocunting Office. *Dislocated Workers. Comaprison of Assistance Programs.* GAO/HRD92-153BR, Sept. 1992. Washington, 1992.

[13] Specifically, 94 percent of TAA workers in Michigan participated in training lasting 26 weeks of more compared to 26 percent of the JTPA workers. In New Jersey, 47 percent of TAA workers compared to 19 percent of JTPA workers participated in the longer trainng, and in Texas, 90 percent of TAA workers comapred to 35 percent of JTPA workers participated in the longer training.

The complicated relationship between the comprehensives of a program and its cost-effectiveness can be illustrated by these two extremes. For example, the most comprehensive and most costly program could be cost-effective if the skill levels and service needs for each worker were assessed prior to the provision of services so that program resources could be allocated as efficiently as possible. On the other hand, the least comprehensive and least costly program would not be cost-effective if workers did not benefit form job search assistance or short-term training. While these options are the extremes, they illustrate the range available for creating a new program or revising existing programs.

THE CHANGING SKILL REQUIREMENTS OF MANUFACTURING JOBS

Linda Levine

SUMMARY

The changing skill requirements of jobs have been the subject of considerable interest. Some analysts have pointed out that the most rapidly growing jobs require high skill or educational levels, while at the same time some youngsters entering the labor force lack the basic skills needed for employment. Other analysts acknowledge that changes in the skill requirements of jobs have been occurring only gradually. Nevertheless, both groups arrive at the same conclusion: in order to bolster the rate of productivity growth, thereby maintaining the Nation's high standard of living and its position as a world-class competitor, education and training policies should be changed.

Many observers believe that the mass production process has become less efficient due to bureaucratization and that firms need to get away from the Taylor model, which creates narrowly-defined jobs that require little thought or discretion to perform. A consensus appears to have developed that firms should reduce layers of management and redesign jobs so that nonsupervisory employees can actively participate in the complete work process and can fully utilize their knowledge and judgment. This kind of industrial restructuring is believed to be a promising strategy for older, high-wage industrialized countries to remain competitive and to preserve manufacturing jobs. Not surprisingly, then, this vision of the *high-performance workplace* is most prevalent among manufacturing firms in the United States.

As measured by changes in the occupational mix of employment, the skill requirements of manufacturing jobs have risen somewhat, *on average*, during the past few decades. There is limited evidence, however, that the rate of increase in skill upgrading due to occupational shifts has been slowing and might slow further in the coming years. Based upon examinations of the skill requirements of *individual* jobs in manufacturing industries, it appears that the extent of the skill transformation is uncertain and its direction is mixed: studies have found evidence of varying degrees of upskilling and deskilling; and, they have found evidence of upskilling for some blue-collar workers (e.g., those already with high skills levels) and of deskilling for others (e.g., lesser skilled production workers). In addition, studies have found that computer-based technologies can affect skill requirements differently from one firm to the next depending upon such intervening variables as managerial decisions, market pressures, and organizational culture (e.g., industrial relations).

At the present time, high-performance work organizations are the exception rather than the rule. It appears that the increasing diffusion of microelectronic technologies will not necessarily create high-performance workplaces. Whether employers choose to re-structure themselves into the current vision of high-performance workplaces could well depend upon such intervening variables as management strategies and industrial rela-tions. If current efforts to change educational and training policies succeed in producing a more skilled labor force, but only a minority of firms opt for the high-performance path, then the unintended outcome could be underemployed, disgruntled workers.

****

Since the late 1980s, the changing skill requirements of jobs have been the focus of considerable attention. A number of analysts have pointed out that the most rapidly growing jobs are those associated with fairly high skill or educational levels, while at the same time some youngsters entering the labor force lack the basis skills needed to get and keep a job.[1] Some observers argue that education and training policies -- from K-12 education through corporate training -- should be reexamined and fundamentally changed in order to maintain the Nation's high standard of living and its position as a premier international competitor.[2] Other analysts acknowledge that changes in the skill requirements of jobs have occurred only gradually, but they too argue that "By prepar-ing more Americans for today's jobs we will, at best, perpetuate the nation's current slow rate of productivity growth and the incomes of most American workers will slide."[3]

Many observers believe that the mass production process has become less efficient due to bureaucratization and that work organizations need to get away from the Taylor model, which has created narrowly-defined jobs that can be performed with minimal skills and little discretion.[4] A consensus appears to have developed that firms should restructure by reducing layers of management and be redesigning jobs so that nonsu-pervisory employees can actively participate in the complete work process and can fully utilize their judgment and knowledge. This kind of industrial restructuring, which is believed to enable mass production establishments to upgrade product design and quality as well as to increase product variety, "is now generally regarded as a highly promising strategy for old, industrial high wage economies striving to remain competi-tive in more volatile and crowded world markets, while at the same time trying to pro-tect their employment in manufacturing.[5] Not surprisingly, then, the embodiment of this vision of the *high-performance workplace* is most prevalent in the United States among

[1]For an example of this line of reasoning, see: Johnston, William B. and Arnold E. Packer. *Workforce 2000*. Indi-anapolis, the Hudson Institute, 1987. p. 97-100, 102-103.

[2]Secretary's Commission on Achieving Necessary Skills. *Learning A Living: A Blueprint for High Performance*. Wash., U.S. Govt. Print. Off., April 1992. p.3-15; and, Hornbeck, David W. and Lester M. Salaman. *Human Capital and America's Future*. Baltimore, Johns Hopkins University Press, 1991. 402 p.

[3]Commission on the Skills of the American Workforce. *America's Choice: High Skills or Low Wages!* Rochester, National Center on Education and the Economy, June 1990. p. 25-29.

[4]Ibid., p. 37-40.

[5]Hyman, Richard and Wolfgang Streeck (eds.) *New Technology and Industrial Relations*. Oxford, Basil Blackwell Ltd., 1988. p. 31.

manufacturing establishments, which have been affected most directly by international competitive pressures.[6]

The following analysis addresses a number of questions that underlie the skill transformation, high-performance issue. Have the skill requirements of manufacturing jobs been changing? If so, in which direction and for which jobs? Are skill changes occurring to a greater or lesser extent than in the past? And, what variables appear to affect the development of high-performance work organizations?

PROXIES FOR SKILL LEVEL

To circumvent the lack of data on skill levels, information on the educational attainment and occupational composition of the labor force often are used as proxies. Both these substitutes have drawbacks, however.

If it were found that employers increasingly have been hiring workers with fairly high levels of educational attainment, it might be concluded that employers are doing this in response to increased skill requirements of jobs. But, alternatives exist to explain this finding. Some portion of the growing employment of highly educated workers might be related merely to the increasing availability of workers with more years of schooling and to the decreasing availability of workers with fewer years of schooling.[7] In addition,

> The usefulness of schooling measures [as a proxy for skill level] is limited by such well-known problems as variations in the quality of schooling, both over time and among regions, the use of credentials as a screening mechanism, and inflationary trends in credential and certification requirements. Indeed, there is some empirical evidence that years of schooling of employees may not closely correspond to the actual skill requirements of the jobs they hold.[8]

> Indeed, the fit between the skill capacities of workers and the skill demands of jobs is notoriously "loose" and has been the subject of appreciable study under the rubrics of overeducation and underemployment. Thus, the schooling, training, or wage levels of workers cannot be equated with the skill requirements of work, except under a very restrictive set of assumptions.[9]

Moreover, the use of educational attainment as a proxy for skill requirements may be less appropriate for some occupations than for others. In one study, the correlation between job-based skill and educational attainment measures was substantially lower among nonsupervisory (e.g., blue-collar) than supervisory (e.g., managerial) workers.[10]

---

[6]Secretary's Commission on Achieving Necessary Skills, *Learning a Living: A Blueprint for High Performance*, p. 24.

[7]According to data of the U.S. Bureau of Labor statistics, in 1975, 34 percent of all workers, regardless of industry, had at least some postsecondary education; by 1987, the proportion had risen to 44 percent.

[8]Howell, David R. and Edward N. Wolff. Trends in the Growth and Distribution of Skills in the U.S. Workplace, 1960-1985. *Industrial and Labor Relations Review*, April 1991. p. 488.

[9]Cyert, Richard M. and David C. Mowery (eds.) *The Impact of Technological Change on Employment and Economic Growth*. Cambridge, Mass., Ballinger Publishing Company, 1988. p. 137-138.

[10]Howell and Wolff, *Trends in the Growth and Distribution of Skills in the U.S. Workplace*, p. 489.

A further drawback is that changes in neither the occupational composition of employment nor the educational attainment of workers addresses the issue of the skill requirements of *individual* jobs. Relatively greater employment in white-collar occupations might lead to the conclusion than, *on average*, all jobs have been upskilled because white-collar occupations generally are associated with higher educational requirements than blue-collar and most service occupations.[11] This rather limited conclusion also holds true only if it is assumed that the skill levels of particular occupations remain unchanged over time.

In addition, the skills of a particular job can be upgraded while the worker's educational level remains the same. An employee in a position that has been upskilled might be taught the newly-required skills through on-the-job training or corporate classroom training, neither of which would affect the worker's level of formal education.

EDUCATIONAL ATTAINMENT

Between 1975 and 1987, the latest year for which such data are available, manufacturers expanded by employing considerably more workers who had completed at least a high school education. As shown in Table 1, manufacturing firms increased the number of employees on their payrolls with at least 4 years of college by 92 percent. During the 12-year period, employment of persons with 1-3 years of college grew by 36 percent, and of high school graduates, by 12 percent.

TABLE 1. Highest Level of Schooling Completed by Employees across All Manufacturing Industries, 1975 and 1987

Highest Level of Schooling Completed	Total Manufacturing Employment (000)			Percent Distribution	
	1975	1987	Percent Change	1975	1987
Total	19,541	21,203	8.5	100.0	100.0
Less than 4 years of high school	6,471	4,368	-32.5	33.1	20.6
years of school or less	2,907	1,670	-42.6	14.9	7.9
1-3 years of high school	3,565	2,697	-24.4	18.2	12.7
4 years of high school	8,519	9,526	11.8	43.6	44.9
1-3 years college	2,544	3,466	36.2	13.0	16.4
4 years or more or college	2,007	3,843	91.5	10.3	18.1
4 years of college	1,453	2,646	82.1	7.4	12.5
Median years	12.4	12.7			

Source: U.S. Bureau of Labor Statistics. March supplements to the Current Population Survey.

---

[11]U.S. Library of Congress. Congressional Research Service. *Education and Job Growth*, by Linda LeGrande. CRS Report No. 88-476 E. Wash., July 1, 1988. p. 1-2.

Nonetheless, as shown in Table 1, the median years of schooling completed by manufacturing employees has increased only slightly. The substantial rates of increase in employing workers with relatively high educational attainment were applied to a fairly small employment base. As a consequence, manufacturing industries continue to be staffed predominantly by employees with a little more than 12 years of schooling.

OCCUPATIONAL DISTRIBUTION

The underlying reason for the increased presence of more educated workers in the manufacturing workforce can be found in its changing occupational mix. Using the motor vehicle and equipment industry for illustrative purposes, managerial and professional workers grew from 8 percent to 13 percent of the industry's total employment between 1977 and 1989. (See Table 2.) Technical, sales, and administrative support workers grew, as well, from 8 percent to 11 percent of the industry's total employment. Most of the hiring within this occupational group occurred among technicians.

Although blue-collar workers remain the largest occupational group at manufacturing establishments, their dominance has diminished. As shown in Table 2, more than four-fifths of the motor vehicle and equipment industry's employment was comprised of blue-collar jobs in 1977, but by 1989, blue-collar jobs accounted for less than three-fourths of the total. According to one analyst, U.S. manufacturing industries were "static" until about the 1980s, when -- at the same time that factory automation was beginning to be introduced -- the proportion of production workers (e.g., laborers, machine operators, precision-production, and craft workers) in the auto industry started to trend downward.[12]

The relative employment of blue-collar production workers has not decreased merely because employment growth has been more robust among other occupational groups. Rather, the relative employment of blue-collar workers has decreased at motor vehicle and equipment producers because their absolute number has fallen. (See Table 2.)

The only other occupational group to experience an absolute decrease in employment among motor vehicle and equipment manufacturers was service workers. Some of the decline might be explained by the increased tendency among employers to contract out functions that previously had been performed in-house, such as protective and janitorial services.

In general, then, motor vehicle and equipment manufacturers increasingly have been hiring workers in those occupational groups that typically require a fairly high level of educational attainment. In contrast, they have been cutting back their employment of workers in occupational groups that typically require fewer years of schooling. The change in the occupational distribution of employment at motor vehicle and equipment producers has, as a consequence, raised the level of educational attainment of the industry's workforce *on average*.

More generally speaking, one study found that for the goods-producing sector,[13] increasingly more of the rise in cognitive skill requirements over time was explained by changes in the sector's occupational mix. During the 1960s, 16 percent of the increase in

---

[12]Swyt, Dennis A. The Workforce of U.S. Manufacturing in the Post-Industrial Era. *Technological Forecasting and Social Change*, Nov. 1988. p. 245 and 250.

[13]In the study, the goods-producing sector is defined to encompass agriculture, mining, manufacturing, and utilities.

the complexity of jobs in the good-producing sector was attributable to changes in the sector's employment distribution by occupation.[14] The proportion of the increase in job complexity during the 1970s associated with changes in the sector's occupational staffing pattern rose to 35 percent, and between 1980 and 1985, to 59 percent. The researchers attributed changes in the good-producing sector's occupational mix to three factors, namely, technological change, new management methods, and outsourcing of low-skill operations.[15]

Table 2. Employment in the Motor Vehicles and Equipment Industry
by Occupational Group, 1977 and 1989

Occupational Group	Employment Level		Percent Distribution of Employment	
	1977	1989	1977	1989
All occupations	950,520	861,220	100.0	100.0
White-collar occupations	73,130	112,687	7.7	13.1
Managers & administrators	31,230	41,110	3.3	4.8
Professionals	41,900	71,577	4.4	8.3
Technical, sales & admin. support	77,510	94,933	8.2	11.0
Technicians	13,890	25,603	1.5	3.0
Sales workers	4,710	10,670	0.5	1.2
Admin. support	58,910	58,660	6.2	6.8
Blue-collar occupations	772,840	638,830	81.3	74.2
Service occupations	27,040	14,640	2.8	1.7

Note: The occupational classification system changed between the two time periods shown. Therefore, the data are not strictly comparable. Source: U.S. Bureau of Labor Statistics. Occupational Employment Survey.

The study further concluded that the cognitive skill requirements of jobs in the good-producing sector increased between 1960 and 1985. However, the rate of increase in the average skill level of workers in the goods-producing sector appears to have slowed over time. The researchers found this result puzzling because, during the 25-year period, investment increased in new technologies which, according to case study literature, are thought to raise the growth rate of cognitive skill levels.[16]

Another study also found evidence of skill upgrading due to changes in the occupational mix of employment from the early 1970s through the mid-1980s. Based upon the U.S. Bureau of Labor Statistics' projection of employment change by occupation be-

---

[14]Howell and Wolff, *Trends in the Growth and Distribution of Skills in the U.S. Workplace*, p. 493.

[15]Ibid., p. 500.

[16]Ibid., p. 500.

tween 1988 and 2000, however, the authors expect the extent of skill upgrading across all jobs in the economy to slow considerably.[17]

THE SKILL LEVELS OF INDIVIDUAL JOBS

Based upon the above analysis of occupational employment change, it might be concluded that the greater employment of manufacturing workers in occupations associated with relatively high levels of educational attainment reflects the rising skill requirements of manufacturing jobs. The analysis does not shed any light on skill changes that might have affected *individual* job classifications, however. To address that point, a synthesis of the literature on the changing skill requirements of individual factory jobs follows. Much of the work on the subject takes a case study approach, and therefore may not be generalizable beyond the particular establishments studied.

The application of computer-based technologies to some tasks at manufacturing plants (e.g., the use of robots for welding and of computers for designing) might have affected the employment demand for and skill requirements of certain jobs.[18] It is likely, for example, that at least some portion of the reduced demand for welding machine setters, operators, and tenders can be ascribed to the greater use of computer-aided production technologies: the number of welding machine setters, operators, and tenders employed in manufacturing industries fell from 126,136 in 1986 to 95,443 in 1990.[19] Similarly, it is likely that some of the lessened demand for drafters is due to the increased diffusion of computer-aided design technologies: the number of drafters at manufacturers fell from 125,618 in 1986 to 106,428 in 1990.

In addition to being labor-saving,[20] although not necessarily labor-displacing, technological innovations may reduce the routine, physical, and dangerous aspects of production jobs. Microelectronic technologies also may require that workers have a set of skills different from those that they previously needed to perform their jobs. Rather than the need for good eye-hand coordination when manually operating machine tools, for example, the use of automated tool guidance systems requires

> the ability to instruct and guide machine tools indirectly through programmable machine tool control systems. For some observers this constitutes a form of deskilling; yet it may just as easily be seen as a shift of emphasis from historically valued skills toward a new constellation of skills more consistent with the capabilities of the new technology.[21]

According to a study of metalworking industries, however, in half of the cases management gave the numerical-control (NC) programming responsibilities to programmers

---

[17]Mishel, Lawrence and Ruy A. Teixeira. *The Myth of the Coming labor Shortage.* Wash., Economic Policy Institute, 1990. p. 28-32.

[18]For additional information on the relationship between technology and employment demand in manufacturing industries, see: U.S. Congress. Office of Technology Assessment. *Computerized Manufacturing Automation.* Wash., U.S. Govt. Print. Off., April 1984. p. 101-176.

[19]Unpublished data from the U.S. Bureau of Labor Statistics.

[20]Levy, Robert A. and James M. Jondrow. The Adjustment of Employment to Technical Change in the Steel and Auto Industries. *Journal of Business,* July 1986. p. 481-485, 487.

[21]Hicks, Donald A. *Automation Technology and Industrial Renewal.* Wash., American Enterprise Institute for Public Policy Research, 1986. p. 123-124.

rather than broadening the skill content of conventional machine operators' jobs. In another 19 percent of the plants studied, machine shop supervisors were assigned the parts programming function. Only 21 percent of the time did management assign programming responsibilities to machine operators.[22] Thus, computer-based automation either can deskill or upskill jobs, depending upon such intervening variables as managerial discretion, the nature of the production process (e.g., batch versus mass production), the size of the shop, and the degree to which the technology has been perfected.[23]

The effect a given technology can have on a given job classification may change over time as the technology itself evolves.[24] When NC technology initially was introduced, as noted above, programmers primarily were responsible for parts programming while machine operators were reduced to being machine monitors. Over the years the technology has become simpler to use, and machine operators more often have been given programming responsibilities. The technology, then, at first deskilled the production worker's job and then reskilled it. If and when programming tasks become fully automated, however, the machine operator's job might once again be deskilled.

Another study, which examined how the use of NC machine tools affects skill levels at nonelectrical machinery manufacturers, neither supports the notion that jobs have been deskilled nor upskilled.[25] Based upon the skill index developed for the analysis, it appears that the increased prevalence of NC machine tools over the past 30 years has reduced skill levels across all machine shop occupations by just one percent. Based upon an analysis of wages,[26] there does not appear to be any measurable deterioration in the overall skill level of machine shop workers.

Perhaps more importantly, the researcher found that NC technology had varying effects on the different jobs in machine shops. The diffusion of NC machine tools has reduced employers' reliance upon "the skilled jobs of setter and set-up operator, the semi-skilled job of machine operator, and the unskilled job of machine tender. The most highly skilled craft workers, tool and die makers, machinists, and tool room operators, however, have not been adversely affected by NC."[27]

Alternatively, a draft report funded by the U.S. Department of Education concluded that there has been considerable upskilling of factory jobs. According to the study's author,

> Some of the changes [in skill requirements] are quite large, as with "Inspection/Quality Control" and "Material Handling." Similarly, some of the changes in the composition of the workforce are also sizable. The

[22]Ibid., p. 124-125. Note: The remaining 10 percent of the time, management gave the programming responsibilities to outside contractors (1 percent) and others (7 percent), or provided no response (2 percent).

[23]Zicklin, Gilbert. Numerical Control Machining and the Issue of Deskilling. *Work and Occupations*, Aug. 1987. p. 462.

[24]U.S. Congress. Office of Technology Assessment. *Worker Training: Competing in the New International Economy.* Wash., U.S. Govt. Print. Off., 1990. p. 122-123.

[25]Keefe, Jeffrey H. Numerically Controlled Machine Tools and Worker Skills. *Industrial and labor Relations Review*, April 1991. p. 514-515.

[26]According to Howell and Wolff, *Trends in the Growth and Distribution of Skills* (p. 490), however, "the use of relative earnings as a proxy for...skill requirements is particularly questionable at the industry level (for all workers), and for nonsupervisory workers at the occupation level. [This is] consistent with the view that labor markets are less competitive for production workers than for professional, technical, and managerial workers, and that industry characteristics play a major role in production worker wage determination."

[27]Keefe, *Numerically Controlled Machine Tools and Worker Skills*, p. 516.

sharp decline in [the number of] "Quality Control" and "Material Handling" (inventory) jobs, for example, may be the result of job redesign efforts that try to incorporate these functions into other jobs. It could be that the functions that remain for workers in quality control have become more highly skilled as a result of transferring the more routine quality functions to other jobs. The rise of "just-in-time" inventory systems, which push some of the material handling functions off to suppliers, may have had a similar effect on jobs in that family.[28]

Although it is difficult to explain this trend toward upskilling because of the aggregate nature of the data, the analyst thought that the use of new production technologies has played a fairly small role. Instead, he tentatively suggested that

> Changes in production jobs seem much more driven by developments in traditional employee relations areas -- new management views concerning how jobs should be redesigned and the decline of union power that made their implementation possible.[29]

This hypothesis relates back to the importance of intervening or conditioning variables, which were mentioned above, in determining whether a particular kind of change upgrades, downgrades, or basically leaves unchanged a job's skill level. Such factors as managerial discretion (e.g., in determining whether and how jobs are redesigned), market pressures, and organizational culture (e.g., industrial relations) can intervene to affect the nature of the skill transformation as well as the definition of a "skilled" job itself.[30]

> [I]n the steel and automobile industries, what comes to be defined as "skilled" in relation to job titles, classifications and hierarchies is some complicated mixture of the technical features of tasks, the past and present of union-management negotiations over job classification systems, and even day-to-day politics of performance-norm definition, worker-supervisor interactions, and other group dynamics.[31]

The findings from a case study of the General Motors' assembly plant in Linden, New Jersey reinforce this same point, that is, the importance of conditioning variables in determining how technological and other changes affect the skill content and skill level of jobs. The findings also reinforce the differential effect of computer-based technological change by occupational category. The researchers concluded that the technological changes at the auto factory (e.g., introduction of robots for use in painting operations and automated guided vehicles for carrying car bodies to the work stations)

---

[28]Capelli, Peter. *Are Skill Requirements Rising? Evidence from Production and Clerical Jobs.* Draft. Wash., U.S. Department of Education, Nov. 14, 1991, p. 25-26.

[29]Ibid., p. 31.

[30]Cyert and Mowery, *The Impact of Technological Change on Employment and Growth*, p. 161-167.

[31]Ibid., 166.

had highly polarized effects on the work force: Skilled trades workers experienced skill upgrading and gained enhanced responsibilities, while production workers underwent deskilling and became increasingly subordinated to the new technology. Reinforcing the turn in recent literature away from technological determinism and toward a "contingency" approach that emphasizes the interaction between technological and social factors, we suggest that the skill polarization at GM-Linden resulted as much from the plant's organizational structure as from technological change itself.[32]

The results of the GM-Linden case study also agree with those of a previously-cited study, which found that the employment of quality inspectors and materials handlers decreased across all manufacturing industries. In the GM-Linden case study, the finding was attributed to the introduction at the auto plant of the build-in-station concept, in which the production workers themselves became responsible for inspecting their work, and to the just-in-time inventory system, in which inventory and therefore personnel requirements were reduced.[33]

In contrast, the employment of skilled trades workers (e.g., electricians) at GM-Linden increased due to the need for them to maintain the new, high-tech machinery. As the increase in employment of these craft workers occurred at the same time that the plant's total employment decreased, they became a larger share of the workforce. Thus, as measured by the changed occupational mix, the skill requirements for workers at the plant increased *on average*.[34]

Although the basic tasks (i.e., job content) of blue-collar occupations remained largely the same at GM-Linden, the skill levels of craft workers rose because of their maintenance of the complex, high-tech machines. conversely, the skill levels of production-line employees fell somewhat, "partly because the new technology eliminated many of the most demanding jobs, and partly because management abolished tag relief and reduced the amount of repair work [by returning rather than repairing defective parts].[35] The latter management changes meant that there was less need for workers in two fairly high-skilled production classifications, namely, relief, "which demands the ability to perform a large number of different jobs, and repair work, which inherently requires greater skill than most production-line jobs."[36] Thus, the traditional skill differences between craft and production workers were exacerbated by the microelectronic technologies, management's decision to reduce the amount of repair work, and the lack of change in workers' job content.[37]

If, along with its decision to modernize the plant, management also had decided to make changes in organizational structure and job content, the skill levels of production workers' jobs might not have fallen.

---

[32]Milkman, Ruth and Cydney Pullman. Technological Change in an Auto Assembly Plant. *Work and Occupations*, May 1991. p. 123-124.

[33]Ibid., p. 129-131.

[34]Ibid., p. 133-134.

[35]Ibid., p. 134.

[36]Ibid., p. 141.

[37]Ibid., p. 143-144.

The deskilling of tasks need not result in deskilled jobs or downgraded workers. Tasks that have been simplified, or deskilled, can often be regrouped to generate jobs requiring similar or more advanced skills than prior to the change, rather than allowing jobs to become more narrow, easier and less satisfying. The use of job rotation and work teams, for instance, results in different skill needs of workers than does the decision to assign a smaller set of specific tasks to individual workers.[38]

At the Linden, New Jersey plant of General Motors, however, management kept much the same organizational structure: it neither reduced the number of job classifications, which would have broadened the remaining classifications' job content, nor introduced flexible work teams, which would have at the least increased the interactive skills of team members.[39] As a consequence, the tasks assigned to production workers after the modernization remained much the same as before,[40] and their skill levels suffered.

In contrast with the experience at GM-Linden, the AC Rochester plant of General Motors introduced organizational changes along with a new production process and technology in 1985.[41] Some 112 classifications for production jobs were reduced to 3. Employees, about one-fourth of whom did not have high school degrees, were retrained so that they could perform the wider range of tasks assigned to the new job classifications. This type of organizational structure, namely, a few broadly-defined and therefore multiskilled production occupations, reflects the job design at Japanese automotive transplants and other Japanese-owned or joint-venture enterprises,[42] but it is not as yet widespread among U.S. automakers.[43]

There is evidence that the high-performance work model is spreading, however.[44] The Sharonville, Ohio plant of Ford Motor Company, for example, adopted a work team approach in 1985, which included going to a single job classification and a pay-for-knowledge compensation system.[45] Within their departments, team members rotate assignments, thereby enabling them to become multiskilled and earn higher pay. The teams, which include a salaried supervisor and an elected coordinator from among the team's hourly employees, are self-managed, that is, each allocates personnel and schedules vacations; meets daily production, schedules, quality standards, and budgets for tools, materials, and scrap; decides their own training needs; discusses and resolve problems; develops plans to achieve goals; and administers the pay-for-knowledge system. The hourly workers received extensive training in both technical areas (e.g., computer-numerical-control machining, blueprint reading, metrics and math, and statistical

[38]Commission on Workforce Quality and Labor Market Efficiency. *Investing in People*, Background Papers. Wash., U.S. Govt. Print. Off., Sept. 1989. p. 428.

[39]Ibid., p. 127.

[40]Ibid., p. 135.

[41]Commission on the Skills of the American Workforce, America's Choice: High Skills or Low Wages!. p. 111.

[42]Kenney, Martin and Richard Florida. How Japanese Industry is Rebuilding the Rust Belt. *Technology Review*, Feb./Mar. 1991. p. 26-27, 31.

[43]Singleton, Christopher J. Auto Industry Jobs in the 1980's: a Decade of Transition. *Monthly Labor Review*, February 1992. p. 24.

[44]For other examples of automotive plants undergoing organizational change, see: Turner, Lowell. Three Plants, Three Futures. *Technology Review*, January 1989. p. 38-45.

[45]Reymond, Renee and Jeanne Sano. *The High Performance Work Force*. Wash., National Association of Manufacturers, 1991. p. 19-22.

process control) and team-building concepts. Union representatives were trained in the workings of self-managed team systems, and managerial personnel were trained in how to make the transition from the hierarchical to the participative style of leadership. As part of the 1982 national collective bargaining agreement with the United Auto Workers, there also is an active, ongoing commitment to help bargaining unit members further upgrade their skills.

Although restructured firms in which workers independently solve technical problems, regularly learn new tasks, and interact frequently with co-workers have garnered considerable attention, these *high-performance workplaces* are not the norm.[46] While some firms have adjusted to international competition and technological change by upgrading job skills to a fairly high level, the fact they are not the majority of firms implies that other firms might have adjusted to these same factors "by altering production in ways that leave job structure intact or even by 'dumping down' new technologies so they can be adapted to existing managerial practices and the perceived quality of the workforce."[47]

Conditioning variables might explain why some firms choose to adapt technology to existing workforce skills while others choose the high-performance path of upgrading workers' skills. One analysis of 21 metalworking industries found, for example, that although management sometimes did assign NC programming responsibilities to blue-collar workers in machining occupations, it did so considerably less often in unionized workplaces and in nonunion workplaces where seniority rules governed promotions and job assignments.[48] This pattern might have developed because management can maintain control and not negotiate about who will do programming and how it will be done, if management initially assigns the new programming function to someone outside the bargaining unit or not otherwise covered by seniority rules.[49] Although anti-union animus did not necessarily underlie management's decision in these task assignments, labor-management relations since the 1980s have not been cordial.[50]

The organizational environment that appears to promote the best chance for upskilling of blue-collar occupations is one in which programmable automation *recently* has been introduced, a joint employee-employer committee exists, and a union is present.[51] With this combination, the chance of redesigning blue-collar jobs to include programming was found to be more than one-third better than the chances of upskilling blue-collar jobs when there is neither a union present nor a joint committee, and more than one-fifth better when there is no union present but there is a joint committee. This finding might

---

[46]Mishel and Teixeira, *The Myth of the Coming Labor Shortage*, p. 36-37; and, Hoerr, John with Michael A. Pollock and David E. Whiteside. Management Discovers the Human Side of Automation. *Business Week*, Sept. 26, 1986. p. 72.

[47]Mishel and Teixeira, *The Myth of the Coming Labor Shortage*, p. 37.

[48]Kelley, Maryellen R. Unionization and Job Design Under Programmable Automation. *Industrial Relations*, Spring 1989. p. 175, 178-183.

[49]For a discussion of how seniority-based work rules can affect job assignments, see: Conti, Robert. Work Practice Barriers to Flexible Manufacturing in the US and the UK. *New Technology, Work and Employment*, Spring 1992. p. 7-8, 12.

[50]Commission on Workforce Quality and Labor Market Efficiency, *Investing in People*, p. 1873-1874.

[51]Kelley, *Unionization and Job Design Under Programmable Automation*, p. 183-184.

reflect the success of a new bargaining strategy among unions participating in joint problem-solving with management, taking place outside
the traditional arena of collective bargaining...The union may be able to
achieve changes in management practices that otherwise could not be
successfully pursued (or codified) through the usual collective bargaining process. Management may be able to get agreement from the union
(or from particular groups of workers within the union membership) to
change work rule practices without having to work out new contract
language.[52]

Unions, for their part, generally have been ambivalent about the value of participating in technology planning with management and about supporting either job redesign
or employee participation.[53] This ambivalence partly might stem from a split in union
ranks between "co-operatists" and "militants."[54] There is some indication, however, that
organized labor now might want to become a more active participant in technology
planning as it affects union members in the workplace.[55]

Just as the organizational culture (e.g., industrial relations) appears to affect whether
a firm chooses the high-performance path, so too does managerial discretion. If a company's competitive strategy mainly focuses on short-run cost reduction, it is unlikely to
be interested in job redesign, which typically requires expenditures for (re)training employees.[56] Similarly, if a company invests in technology for the purpose of cutting employment or gaining more control over workers, it is likely to discourage rather than
encourage employee participation in the work process. Alternatively, if a company
adopts a competitive strategy that emphasizes product quality as ell as fast and flexible
responses to the changing preferences of customers, it might have an interest in developing adaptable, multi skilled workers. In addition, if a company recognizes the importance of the social dimension in achieving optimal use of computer-based technologies,
it is likely to be attentive to human resource (e.g., job redesign, work teams, and retraining) and other organizational (e.g., management style) issues.[57]

SUMMARY AND CONCLUSIONS

As measured by shifts in the occupational composition of employment toward greater
reliance upon managerial, professional, and technical workers, the skill requirements of
jobs in manufacturing industries have risen somewhat, *on average*, during the past few
decades. There is some evidence to suggest that the rate of increase in skill upgrading
associated with changes in the occupational mix of jobs has been slowing, however.

---

[52]Ibid. p. 185-186.

[53]Commission on Workforce Quality and Labor Market Efficiency, *Investing in People*, p. 1872; and Hoerr, *Management Discovers the Human Side of Automation*, p. 75. For information on employee participation and labor relations in the auto industry, see: Hyman and Streeck, *New Technology and Industrial Relations*, p. 101-127; and in
glass industry, see: Swoboda, Frank. Partnership with Union Produces Results. *Washington Post*, Aug. 2, 1992. p.
H4.

[54]Hyman and Streeck, *New Technology and Industrial Relations*, p. 220-232.

[55]Swoboda, Frank. Organized Labor Awakening to the Impact of Technology. *Washington Post*, July 26, 1992. p.
H2.

[56]Commission on Workforce Quality and Labor Market Efficiency, *Investing in People*, p. 1869-1871.

[57]Hoerr, *Management Discovers the Human Side of Automation*, p. 70-75.

Based upon a review of the literature on the changing skill requirements of *individual* jobs, it appears that the extent of the skill transformation is uncertain and its direction is mixed. Studies have found evidence of upskilling for certain blue-collar manufacturing workers (e.g., those already possessing fairly high skill levels) and evidence of deskilling for others (e.g., lesser skilled production workers).

And, they have found that the effect of computer-based technological innovations on skill requirements can differ from one firm to the next depending upon conditioning variables, such as managerial decisions, market pressures, and organizational culture. It appears that the increasing diffusion of microelectronic technologies across manufacturing industries will not necessarily result in the creation of high-performance workplaces.

Whether work organizations staffed by flexible, multi skilled employees become the new manufacturing paradigm seems to be associated with such intervening variables as management strategies and labor-management relations. While changes in public education and training policies might upgrade the quality of the labor supplied to employers, employers -- sometimes with the participation of employees and their representatives -- ultimately will be the ones to choose whether or not to restructure themselves into some version of the high-performance workplace. If efforts to improve the quality of students entering the labor force and of workers already in the labor force succeed, while at the same time only a minority of firms take the high-performance path, then an unintended outcome might be underemployed, disgruntled workers.

WORK PROGRAMS FOR WELFARE RECIPIENTS: A LOOK AT PAST EFFORTS

Karen Spar

SUMMARY

Welfare reform is high on the legislative agenda in the 104th Congress. A key related issue is whether the Federal Government has an obligation to provide jobs for welfare recipients who are unable to find work in the private labor market; thus, an examination of past government jobs programs is timely. The largest and best-known jobs programs of the past are those of the New Deal and the public service employment components of the Comprehensive Employment and Training Act (CETA); however, these programs were not targeted exclusively on welfare recipients. Job-creation programs specifically for welfare recipients have generally taken the form of small demonstration projects or optional work experience activities designed largely by States.

Since the New Deal era, society's expectations of who should work, and therefore, who should participate in government-funded jobs programs, has shifted from predominantly men to also include women. Recent proposals to require or encourage welfare recipients to work have focused primarily on poor mothers. At the same time, public support for government jobs programs serving the unemployed in general, rather than exclusively welfare recipients, has diminished. While the New Deal enjoyed generally broad support due to massive unemployment that affected a large segment of the population, the CETA jobs programs of the 1970s were permanently tainted by early allegations of fraud, nepotism and mismanagement. Since the demise of CETA in the early 1980s, efforts to revive a broad-scale public jobs program have been unsuccessful.

As for the value of past programs, the Works Progress Administration (WPA) and the Civilian Conservation Corps (CCC) are credited with long-term contributions to society and to individual participants. Particularly when viewed 50 years later, both of these New Deal programs had a significant impact on the Nation's physical and cultural landscape. They also served large numbers of unemployed people, who likely would have been jobless during the Depression. However, both programs had critics, who charged that WPA projects could have been undertaken at less cost, that WPA recreation projects were frivolous, and that the CCC's education component was of low quality.

The value of CETA's jobs programs changed over time. In the early years, when eligibility criteria were relatively loose and wages could be supplemented with no limit, local governments tended to hire CETA workers for routine government jobs and generally found the program valuable. However, concern developed about worker displacement and Congress amended the program to target jobs on a more disadvantaged population. This reduced the temptation for local officials to substitute CETA workers for regular employees, but also caused a drop in the rate of participant transition into unsubsidized employment, made jobs less useful to local governments, and made jobs less valuable to participants, due to lower wages and shorter duration.

There are no comprehensive national studies of work experience programs designed specifically for welfare recipients. Research conducted in several States in the 1980s found that work experience positions in which recipients received welfare benefits in lieu of wages typically were entry-level jobs. Supervisors found participants' performance comparable to that of regular entry-level workers, but also felt that participants did not gain or improve job skills. Participants, while generally positive, felt their welfare checks were not adequate compensation and would have preferred traditional paid employment.

INTRODUCTION

Welfare reform is high on the legislative agenda in the 104th Congress.[1] A key issue related to welfare reform is whether the Federal Government has an obligation to provide jobs for welfare recipients who are unable to find work in the private labor market. While general support exists for the concept that employable welfare recipients should be required or encouraged to work there is debate as to whether sufficient jobs exist in the private sector for large numbers of workers with low skills and little experience.

The largest government jobs programs of the past were not targeted on welfare recipients, but were created for countercyclical purposes to combat high unemployment during periods of recession. Most well-known are the work programs of the New Deal and the public service employment components of the Comprehensive Employment and Training Act (CETA). These programs were designed at the Federal level in response to perceived national needs. On the other hand, job-creation programs targeted specifically at welfare recipients have generally taken the form of small demonstration projects or optional activities designed largely by States.

This report reviews selected job-creation programs of the past, as well as certain activities for welfare recipients that are still ongoing. The report attempts to answer some of the factual questions frequently asked by policymakers considering new legislation to create public sector jobs. Program descriptions are based on available data and information.

Excluded from this report are post-New Deal public works programs, programs that are considered "volunteer" in nature such as VISTA or national service, and programs that provide incentives to the private sector to create jobs for welfare recipients or other target populations. Also excluded are summer jobs programs for low-income youth, employment programs for low-income elderly, and training programs and other efforts to enhance the employability of welfare recipients that do not actually create jobs. Unless specified, dollar figures have not been adjusted for inflation.

---

1 Legislation is moving through the 104th Congress that would repeal the existing Aid to Families with Dependent Children (AFDC) program and establish a block grant to States for time-limited assistance to needy families with children (H.R. 4). For background information and the status of legislation, see: U.S. Library of Congress. congressional Research Service. Welfare Reform. CRS Issue Brief No. IB93034, by Vee Burke. Regularly updated.

OVERVIEW

A number of trends emerge from the history of public employment programs, some of which reflect changes in society in general. For example, society's expectations of who should work, and therefore, who should participate in government-funded jobs programs, have changed dramatically over the past 60 years. During the 1930s, men were expected to work and support their families while women stayed home to care for children. Thus, when the Depression forced many workers into unemployment, Federal job-creation programs were established primarily for men, while Aid to Dependent Children[2] was authorized to enable women and children without a male breadwinner to be supported at home.

The job-creation programs of the New Deal were temporary and ended with World War II, although public jobs programs were also used in the 1970s as a response to high unemployment. Aid to Families with Dependent Children (AFDC), on the other hand, was enacted as a permanent program and has persisted through numerous social changes, including the massive entry of women into the workforce in recent decades. As the majority of all women with children now work, public support has eroded for a welfare program that enables needy mothers to stay home indefinitely. Therefore, welfare reform debates have increasingly focused on ways to encourage or require others to work or, at a minimum, enroll in school or training.

Several other trends emerge from the history of public jobs programs in addition to the shift in target population. The early employment programs -- those of the New Deal -- were developed in response to extraordinary rates of unemployment that affected a wide spectrum of the population. In general, these programs enjoyed greater public support and less stigma than more recent Federal job-creation efforts. The public employment programs of the 1970s, primarily under CETA, were broadly targeted on the unemployed, but became permanently tainted by early reports of fraud, nepotism and mismanagement. Public support for government-financed public service jobs further diminished as national unemployment rates lowered and as Congress increasingly targeted the program on a narrower portion of the unemployed population, i.e., the poor and unskilled.

Since the demise of CETA in the early 1980s, efforts to revive a broad-scale public employment program have been unsuccessful. The impetus for discussions of job-creation has shifted from high national unemployment rates that affect the middle-class, to concern about growth in public welfare programs and development of a permanently dependent "underclass" that many people believe should fulfill their obligation to society by working in exchange for receiving public assistance. Thus, current proposals are more likely to be targeted on "mandatory" populations, such as welfare recipients, and to follow the "workfare" model of work-for-benefits, as opposed to CETA-type programs which were voluntary and paid wages for employment.

Public employment programs have been controversial for various reasons, almost always including their relatively high cost. In addition to their cost, however, these programs have been troubled because of multiple and sometimes conflicting goals, i.e., creating meaningful jobs for unemployed and low-skilled individuals so that they may eventually enter the unsubsidized labor market, while also providing useful services to society in a cost-effective manner, without threatening the existing public sector workforce.

---

[2] Later renamed Aid to Families with Dependent Children.

Experiences of the past have demonstrated the difficulty of simultaneously meeting these goals. For example, the more disadvantaged the target population, the less likely that a program will cause displacement of unsubsidized workers. However, the public value of the work performed may decline and subsequent placement of participants into unsubsidized jobs may be difficult. Further, programs serving individuals with low skills and little experience may require a greater investment of training, supervision, and support services. On the other hand, programs serving a broader spectrum of the workforce are more prone to displacement and may be costly, because of the larger eligible population and the likelihood of higher wages and benefits.

THE NEW DEAL

The New Deal is associated with creation of numerous Federal programs to address the massive unemployment and poverty that occurred during the Great Depression of the 1930s. In addition to the permanent social insurance and public assistance programs enacted under the Social Security Act of 1935, several temporary job-creation programs existed that employed millions of otherwise jobless individuals. These programs ended with the onset of World War II, although there was some support for enactment of a permanent jobs program.

The earliest of the temporary programs were the Civil Works Administration (CWA) and the Federal Emergency Relief Administration (FERA). The CWA existed only for 5 months, from November 1933 to Mach 1934, but employed 4.3 million workers at its peak. The FERA existed from May 1933 to December 1935 and provided both cash welfare benefits (referred to then as "direct relief") and job opportunities (known as "work relief"), employing as many as 1.4 million to 2.4 million individuals per month.

Work-related programs of the New Deal also included the Public Works Administration, the National Youth Administration, and the Reconstruction Finance Corporation. However, two of the best-known programs were the Works Progress Administration (WPA) and the Civilian Conservation Corps (CCC). Modern-day advocates of public jobs programs often cite the long-term contributions of these two programs, both to society as well as to individual participants. The following sections focus specifically on the WPA and the CCC.

WORKS PROGRESS ADMINISTRATION

History and Purpose. The Works Progress Administration was established in 1935 to provide jobs for needy employable individuals on projects throughout the country during a period of extraordinarily high national unemployment. The WPA was renamed the Work Projects Administration in 1939, and ended in 1943.

Program Design. To be eligible for the WPA, individuals had to be "needy" (as determined by local welfare agencies), employable (i.e., physically fit), and, for most of the program's duration, at least 18 years old (prior to July 1938, the minimum age was 16). Only one person in a family could be employed in a WPA job; thus, WPA participants were most often heads of families. Recipients of unemployment compensation were initially excluded from the WPA, although this policy was modified over time to allow participation by workers whose unemployment benefits were relatively small.

Once accepted into the WPA, workers awaited assignment to a project. Because the number of accepted workers always exceeded the number of available jobs, a system of preferences was developed. Initially, veterans received first preference, but in 1939, Congress established preferences based on financial need. Within these need categories, veterans continued to receive preference, and in 1941, veterans' preference was also extended to veterans' widows and wives of unemployed veterans.

Beginning in 1939, workers could not be continuously employed by the WPA for more than 18 months, except for veterans (and, under a later amendment, their widows and wives) who wee exempt from this restriction. Workers were expected to continue their search for unsubsidized employment throughout their participation in the WPA, and were required to be registered with the U.S. Employment Service. In addition to their job, WPA workers received training and job placement services.

Under the FERA program, which preceded the WPA, wages were paid in accordance with the worker's financial need. Under the WPA, it was decided that workers would receive a "security" wage, which would be larger than relief payments, but not high enough to compete with wages in the private sector. The specific amount of wages paid to an individual WPA worker was based on three factors: the worker's skill level; the geographic region; and degree of urbanization in the area. Although the amounts paid to each individual worker varied, the average security wage was $50 per month per worker.

Early in the WPA's history, there was concern that the program's low payment rates might depress wages in the private sector. Thus, it was decided that WPA workers could be paid, per hour, the prevailing rate paid to private sector workers in the same geographic regions. However, since the total amount received by an individual worker could not exceed the security wage, this policy required that higher wage workers work fewer hours. The resulting inefficiency led to abandonment of the prevailing rate of pay policy in 1939.

The WPA provided construction and engineering jobs, as well as employment in the service sector. Service projects represented about a fourth of WPA employment during the program's first 5 and a half years, and rose to half of all WPA jobs by the program's end. Service jobs were provided in a wide variety of areas, including adult education, nursery schools, library services, recreation projects, museum projects, writing, art, theater, conducting social and economic surveys and studies, research assistance, collecting public and historical records, sewing projects, preparation of school lunches, gardening and canning projects, housekeeping projects, public health and hospital projects.

Size and Scope. In 8 years of existence, the WPA provided employment to about 8.5 million individuals, of whom between half and three-quarters were classified as unskilled. Because most of these individuals were heads of families, it was estimated that one-fourth of all families were supported by a WPA job at one time or another during the program's 8 years. The average monthly enrollment peaked in November 1938, at 3.3 million workers.

Because the WPA gave preference for jobs to veterans and household heads, young people and women did not constitute a large proportion of the workers. Older individuals (aged 45 or older) always comprised at least one-third of WPA workers, and were two-thirds of the WPA workforce by the program's last year. Until mid-1941, women comprised between 12% and 18% of WPA workers. However, their proportion increased to 22% by the end of 1941, and to 40% a year later, as the improving private sector and growing military offered new opportunities for men. Blacks constituted 14% of WPA workers in early 1939 and 20% by the end of 1942.

Expenditures for the WPA totaled almost $13 billion, of which $10.1 billion was Federal and $2.8 billion was provided by State and local government "sponsors." Of Federal WPA funds, 89% was spent on wages, while 83% of the State and local sponsor contributions was used for materials, supplies and equipment, and other nonlabor costs. WPA projects provided almost 14 million person-years of employment, at an average cost per person-year of $941.

Accomplishments and Evaluations. Supporters of the WPA point out the numerous achievements of the program during its 8 years, including the construction or improvement of hundreds of thousands of roads, buildings, water and sewer facilities, sidewalks, parks, playgrounds and stadiums. Millions of feet of airport runways were built or improved, and 200 million trees were planted in public forests throughout the country.

In the service sector, WPA workers produced millions of clothing garments, including institutional garments such as hospital gowns. More than a billion school lunches were served, 85 million quarts of food were canned, 11 million pounds of food were dried, and more than 32 million home visits were made by WPA housekeeping aides. Hundreds of thousands of people participated in WPA-sponsored adult education courses, nursery schools, and music performances.

Although displacement was raised as an issue in the 1930s, the WPA's low wage rates and types of projects (services and public works that would not have been undertaken otherwise) resulted in little competition with the private sector.

Particularly when viewed 50 years later, the accomplishments of the WPA had a significant impact on the landscape and culture of the United States. However, evidence indicates that some of the construction projects performed by the WPA could have been undertaken at less cost through contracts with private builders. Likewise, the WPA's cultural and recreation projects were highly controversial at the time and seen by many as frivolous government spending. Advocates of the WPA argued that the program's costs were outweighed by the value to the individual worker, who might otherwise have been idle while receiving cash assistance. Further, recreation programs were endorsed by their supporters as crime prevention activities, as well as opportunities for unemployed artists and other workers.

CIVILIAN CONSERVATION CORPS

History and Purpose. The Civilian Conservation Corps began in 1933 with two general goals: to provide work experience for unemployed young men; and to promote conservation of resources. The CCC was formally established as a government agency in 1937, and was terminated in 1942.

Program Design. To become a "junior enrollee" in the CCC, individuals had to be unmarried males, between the ages of 17 and 23 (the original age limits of 18 and 25 were lowered in 1937), unemployed and out of school, physically and mentally healthy, and willing to remain in the Corps for at least 6 months or until a better job was found. In addition, about 10% of CCC participants were war veterans.

The Director of the CCC administered the program with the assistance of the Departments of War, Interior and Agriculture, and the Veterans Administration. Corpsmembers were assigned to residential camps where a military-type schedule was followed, including 8 hours of work each weekday, plus educational and recreational activities in the evenings. Enrollees were paid $30 per month, consisting of $8 in cash, a $15 allotment to their dependents (if they had any), and $7 that were held and returned upon discharge. In addition, Corpsmembers received food, shelter, clothing, personal supplies, education programs and medical care.

Size and Scope. During its nearly 9 years of existence, the CCC enrolled slightly more than 3 million men, of which 95% came from families that were considered underprivileged. About 90% of Corpsmembers were between the ages of 17 and 20; 80% had never worked or had worked only for short spells; and 30% had not completed grade school. The CCC cost approximately $3 billion, with an annual per enrollee cost of about $1,000. The largest single expenditure was for cash allowances to enrollees. The program operated throughout the Continental United States, plus Hawaii, Alaska, Puerto Rico and the Virgin Islands.

Accomplishments and Evaluations. As with the WPA, the physical accomplishments of the CCC were vast. Two billion trees were planted by Corpsmembers throughout the United States; 25 million acres of land were protected from soil erosion; 4 million acres of forest land were thinned and improved; and almost a billion fish were stocked. In addition to conservation work, the CCC improved landscape and recreation areas, and built thousands of buildings, bridges, fences, telephone lines, sewage and waste-disposal systems, water supply systems, and roads.

Benefits to Corpsmembers, in addition to cash allowances, included education and health gains. Of 3 million Corpsmembers during the life of the program, 90% participated in organized classes and activities, and 100,000 previously illiterate men were taught to read and write. About 25,000 enrollees received eighth grade diplomas while enrolled in the Corps; 5,000 received high school diplomas; and college degrees were awarded to 270 individuals. However, despite the widespread participation of Corpsmembers, the education program was a controversial component of the CCC and was attacked as being of limited value and low quality. State and local educators were particularly critical of the ability of the Army, which administered the camps, to provide meaningful education services.

THE COMPREHENSIVE EMPLOYMENT AND TRAINING ACT (CETA)

PUBLIC SERVICE EMPLOYMENT COMPONENTS

History and Purpose. The Comprehensive Employment and Training Act (CETA) was enacted in 1973 to consolidate what was then considered a proliferation of categorical programs authorized under the Economic Opportunity Act and the Manpower Development and Training Act. CETA was also designed to decentralize delivery of employment and training services from the Federal to the local level, and was administered through a nationwide network of about 450 local government prime sponsors.

CETA authorized job training and related services for structurally unemployed, low-income individuals. As an adjunct to training in areas with substantial unemployment, the original Act included a program of transitional public service jobs for structurally unemployed workers under title II. However, one year after its enactment, CETA was amended to include a countercyclical public service employment program, developed in response to a sharply escalating national unemployment rate. This program was authorized under a new title VI of the Act. (an earlier countercyclical employment program, authorized by the Emergency Employment Act of 1972, had been allowed to expire when the jobless rate dropped in 1973.)

Spending for countercyclical public service jobs under title VI grew dramatically and quickly outstripped the title II program for the disadvantaged. However, as public service employment grew, so did concerns about fraud and abuse, worker displacement and fiscal substitution. Amendments enacted in 1978 attempted to re-establish CETA's emphasis on low-income, structurally unemployed workers, and to eliminate potential for abuse and mismanagement. Although subsequent evaluations indicated that these amendments were generally effective in accomplishing their goals, the program's negative public image prevailed. Public service employment under CETA was phased out and eliminated in 1981, and in 1982, CETA was replaced with the Job Training Partnership Act, which authorized training for economically disadvantaged individuals and specifically prohibited use of funds for public service jobs.

Program Design. Under the original CETA, individuals eligible for public service jobs under title II had to be unemployed 30 days or more, or be underemployed. However, within this overall guideline, the program was intended to be targeted on the most severely disadvantaged in terms of the length of their unemployment and their prospects for obtaining a job. Vietnam veterans and former training program participants also received priority.

To be eligible for public service jobs under title VI, as originally enacted in 1974, workers also had to be unemployed 30 days or more, or be underemployed. However, in areas with unemployment rates of 7% or higher, individuals could be unemployed a minimum of only 15 days instead of 30. Targeting provisions included those under title II (i.e., the most severely disadvantaged, Vietnam veterans, former trainees), but also included unemployed workers who had exhausted their unemployment compensation benefits, unemployed workers not eligible for unemployment compensation (except for new entrants into the labor force), individuals unemployed 15 weeks or more, and veterans who had separated from the military within the past 4 years.

In 1976, Congress attempted to increase participation by disadvantaged workers in the countercyclical title VI program. Amendments passed that year established additional eligibility and targeting provisions that applied to half of any vacancies that existed as of June 1976, and to new positions. Under these provisions, workers had to be from a low-income family; a recipient of unemployment compensation for at least 15 weeks; unemployed at least 15 weeks but not eligible for unemployment compensation; an exhaustee of unemployment benefits; or an AFDC recipient.

Finally, in 1978, Congress amended both the title II and title VI programs to target service more emphatically on low-income workers. Individuals eligible for the newly established title II-D program for the economically disadvantaged had to be unemployed 15 weeks *and* be a member of a low-income family, or receive AFDC or Supplemental Security Income (SSI). Services were further targeted on the most severely disadvantaged, with special consideration for Vietnam veterans, public assistance recipients, and people with labor market disadvantages such as offenders, limited English speakers, the disabled, women, single parents, displaced homemakers, youth, older workers, and people lacking educational credentials.

Eligibility for the amended title VI program was limited to unemployed workers who had been jobless at least 10 of the previous 12 weeks, *and* who were either AFDC or SSI recipients or members of a low-income family. The same targeting criteria established for the title II-D program described above, also applied to the amended title VI.

As originally enacted, neither of CETA's public service employment programs limited the length of time a participant could remain in a subsidized job, although jobs were intended to be transitional and eventually lead to unsubsidized work. Workers were paid the higher of either the minimum wage or the prevailing rate of pay for comparable jobs. Wages supported with Federal funds could not exceed an annual level of $10,000

($7,800 was established as the desired annual average wage level nationwide), although employers could supplement wages from non-Federal sources.

In an effort to reduce the program's potential for worker displacement, the 1976 amendments required that "new" hires in the title VI program, above the level of CETA workers then employed, must be assigned to projects that could last no longer than one year. These projects were supposed to result in a specific product or goal that could not have been accomplished without Federal funds, and were intended to limit the ability of State or local government agencies to substitute CETA workers for regular employees. The 1976 amendments did not limit the duration of an individual's employment under CETA or address wage rates.

The 1978 amendments, along with tightening eligibility requirements for CETA jobs, established a limit on participation of 18 months in a 5-year period under both title II-D and title VI. Waivers allowing an additional 12 months could be granted by the Labor Department in areas with unemployment rates of at least 7% if it was particularly difficult to place workers in unsubsidized jobs. In addition, the 1978 amendments allowed adjustment of the maximum Federal wage from $10,000 to $12,000 in high-wage areas, but prohibited any further supplementing of wages for workers hired after September 1978. Moreover, the national average annual wage level was reduced from $7,800 to $7,200.

Size and Scope. During approximately 7 years, CETA provided public service jobs for more than 8 million individuals, including about 1.5 million in title II and more than 6.6 million in title VI. Total Federal outlays for public service employment under CETA were about $23 billion ($7.8 billion under title II and $15.3 billion under title VI). Federal costs per person were somewhat less than $3,000; however, Federal costs per *service-year* (one full-time position funded for 1 year, which could have been filled by more than one person) were almost $9,000. Under the titles II and VI programs combined, almost 2.6 million service-years were supported.

As indicated above, public service jobs went to a more disadvantaged population in CETA's later years than during the first few years of the Act. During 1975 through 1977 (prior to implementation of the 1976 and 1978 amendments), about two-thirds of job-holders under both title II and title VI were men; about three-quarters were high school graduates; about two-thirds were white; slightly less than half were economically disadvantaged; and fewer than 10% were AFDC recipients. By 1981, about half the enrollees in both programs were men; high school graduates had dropped to two-thirds of enrollees; half were white; more than 90% were economically disadvantaged, and 20% of title II-D enrollees and 15% of title VI workers were recipients of AFDC when they entered the program.

Accomplishments and Evaluations. Because CETA underwent significant and frequent amendments, the value of its public service employment programs -- both for local communities and for individual participants -- changed over time. During the program's early years, when eligibility criteria were relatively loose and wages could be supplemented with no limit, prime sponsors tended to hire CETA workers for routine local government jobs, providing basic and necessary services. Local governments generally found CETA workers to be most valuable during this period in the program's evolution.

As already stated, concern developed during this period about worker displacement, mismanagement and abuse. Although later evaluations found the displacement was never as significant as originally thought, the 1978 amendments successfully targeted the program on a more disadvantaged population and reduced the temptation for local officials to substitute CETA workers for regular public sector employees. These amendments restored program integrity, but achieved this goal at a price. The shift toward less skilled and more disadvantaged participants, coupled with a worsening economy, resulted in a drop in the rate of participant transition in unsubsidized employment after the CETA job ended. The lower skill level of PSE enrollees also caused jobs to be less useful to local government sponsors, and the lower wages and shorter duration of the jobs made then less useful to participants.

As for the impact of public service employment on participants' later earnings, follow-up studies found that women and workers with the lowest pre-program earnings showed the largest earnings gains, primarily because of greater hours of employment rather than increased wage levels. These findings are similar to evaluations of CETA training programs for economically disadvantaged individuals.

WORK PROGRAMS FOR WELFARE RECIPIENTS

The post-New Deal history of public employment programs created specifically for welfare recipients consists of a series of small programs that began as optional activities for States in the early 1960s. The Community Work and Training (CWT) program was authorized under the Social Security Act in 1962, and allowed States to require individuals to perform "constructive work" in exchange for their welfare grants. This program was largely intended for unemployed men in States that paid AFDC benefits to two-parent households, which was a new option for States at that time. Only 13 states chose to participate in CWT at its peak in 1965. In 1964, the Economic Opportunity Act authorized a Work Experience Program under Title V that was similar to CWT, but provided more generous Federal funding and was not strictly limited to welfare recipients, although more than half of participants did receive AFDC.

Both these early initiatives were replaced in 1967 with enactment of the Work Incentive (WIN) program under the Social Security Act. WIN represented a change in Federal policy in that, for the first time, all "appropriate" AFDC recipients were required to participate, thereby shifting the program's target population to women, who are the vast majority of AFDC recipients. in 1971, Congress ended the ability of States to determine who was appropriate, and required that all AFDC recipients must participate in WIN unless they were exempt for some reason established in Federal law (such as having a preschool-aged child).

Because of statutory exemptions from participation and funding limitations, less than half of adult AFDC recipients were required to register for WIN and less than half of those registered actually received services. Although public service employment and work experience were intended to be components of WIN, participants were more likely to receive less expensive services, such as classroom training or job search assistance. in 1981, Congress enacted the Omnibus Budget Reconciliation Act (OBRA) which allowed States to use their WIN grants to operate demonstration programs of their own design, and also amended the AFDC program to allow States to operate several additional work-related activities, including Community Work Experience Programs (CWEP).

Congress repealed WIN altogether in 1988 with enactment of the Family Support Act, which established a new education, training and employment program for welfare recipients called JOBS (Job Opportunities and Basic Skills). Under JOBS, welfare recipients with children as young as 3 (or age 1, at State option) may be required to participate in a work-related activity. States must develop an employability plan for each JOBS participant and must offer a range of education and training services, job readiness, job development and job placement activities, and supportive services. States must offer at least two of the following four: job search, on-job training, work supplementation (in which AFDC benefits are used to subsidize employment in the private or non-profit sector), and CWEP or an alternative work experience program. The following sections focus on CWEP.

COMMUNITY WORK EXPERIENCE PROGRAM

History and Purpose. As described above, Congress amended AFDC in 1981 to *allow* States to operate several work-related activities, including CWEP projects in which AFDC recipients could be required to work in exchange for their welfare benefits. In 1988, Congress created JOBS, which *requires* States to operate at least two of four work-related activities, of which CWEP is one.

As a component of JOBS, CWEP is intended to be part of an overall welfare-to-work strategy that may also include education and training, job search assistance, supportive services or other activities designed to enhance the employability of welfare recipients. As stated in the law, the purpose of CWEP is to provide actual work experience and training for individuals not otherwise able to obtain employment, to help them move into an unsubsidized job. CWEP serves the purpose of establishing a reciprocal obligation, in which the welfare recipient makes a contribution to society in exchange for a publicly funded benefit.

Program Design. Unlike other programs described in this report, CWEP is *authorized* by Federal law, but is *designed and administered* by State welfare agencies. Thus, with the exception of certain basic Federal requirements, the specific features of CWEP programs vary among States that choose to operate them.

CWEP projects must serve a useful public purpose in such fields as health, social service, environmental protection, education, urban and rural development and redevelopment, welfare, recreation, public facilities, public safety, and day care. States are supposed to consider any prior training, experience or skills that a recipient may have when making CWEP assignments. After every CWEP assignment, and at least every 6 months, the State welfare agency must reassess each participant and revise, if necessary, their employability plan.

The maximum number of hours an individual can be required to participate in CWEP is determined by dividing the family's AFDC benefit by the Federal or State minimum wage, whichever is higher. After the first 9 months in a particular CWEP assignment, an individual cannot be required to continue in the same assignment unless the number of hours worked is calculated by dividing the AFDC benefit by the prevailing rate of pay for a comparable job (or minimum wage, if higher).

Size and Scope. As already discussed, legislation enacted in 1981 established CWEP as an option for States, and by 1988, 30 States were operating some type of CWEP program, although few were conducted statewide. After enactment of the Family Support Act in 1988, States continued to have the option of operating CWEP, and as of January 1994, 35 States did so. However, as a component of the overall JOBS program, CWEP is small, enrolling only 4.3% of all JOBS participants in FY1993 (and accounting for 3% of JOBS expenditures in FY1992).

The total number of CWEP enrollees during FY1993 was about 23,000. characteristics of these enrollees indicate some differences from the larger population of all JOBS participants. For example, CWEP enrollees were more likely to have completed high school (47%, compared with 39% of all JOBS participants). CWEP enrollees also were some-

what older (only 12% of CWEP enrollees were 20 or younger, compared with 31% of all
JOBS participants; 40% of CWEP enrollees were 35 or older, compared with 27% of all
JOBS participants). CWEP enrollees were more likely to be white (66%, compared with
48% of all JOBS participants); included a greater proportion of men (27%, compared
with 14% of all JOBS participants); and had older children (21% of CWEP enrollees had
a youngest child under age 3, compared with 35% of JOBS participants, while 54% of
CWEP enrollees had a youngest child age 6 or older, compared with 36% of JOBS participants).

Accomplishments and Evaluations. As stated above, States vary in their design and
administration of CWEP. Further, while States have been authorized to operate CWEP
or some form of unpaid work experience since 1981, the program has served a small
percentage of welfare recipients nationwide. Thus, there are no comprehensive national
studies of the impact and effectiveness of CWEP as a welfare-to-work strategy. The following summarizes findings of the Manpower Demonstration Research Corporation
(MDRC), which conducted extensive evaluations of welfare-to-work programs in the
1980s and early 1990s, including nine with significant unpaid work experience[3] components. Eight of the programs were conducted under the WIN demonstration authority
provide in OBRA of 1981, and one was conducted under JOBS. Therefore, these findings
for the most part apply to programs operated before implementation of the Family Support Act.

Most of the evaluations conducted by MDRC were small-scale. With one exception,
the programs offered unpaid work experience as one of several program components,
and typically provided unpaid work experience only to a small portion of eligible participants. Duration in work experience was typically 12 to 13 weeks, although participants sometimes were reassigned to a subsequent position. (This short duration may
have been a function of WIN program rules in some cases, as well as other factors.)

Based on research conducted at six programs in the 1980s, MDRC found that unpaid
work experience positions typically were entry-level jobs in maintenance, clerical work,
park service or human services. Supervisors in these six programs considered the work
to be important and found that participants' performance was comparable to regular
entry-level workers. However, supervisors also felt that participants did not gain or improve job skills as a result of their work experience. Participants in the programs were
positive about the experience and felt they made a useful contribution; however, they
also felt their welfare checks were not adequate compensation for the work and would
have preferred traditional paid employment.

MDRC was able to isolate the effects of unpaid work experience in three studies, but
only one found a consistent significant increase in participants' employment and earnings. Further, the effect of unpaid work experience on welfare receipt and amount of
welfare payments was inconsistent among the three programs. In two programs that
offered work experience in conjunction with job search, small but significant reductions
in welfare receipt and payments were found, but these reductions were not statistically
different from the effects of job search alone. In the third program, a small but significant decrease in welfare receipt among women was found at 21 months after participation but not in longer-term studies. For men in this program, consistent significant reductions in welfare receipt and payments were found, but researchers cautioned that
this may have been due to factors that could not be controlled statistically. MDRC suggested that, based on several of their other studies, unpaid work experience might be

---

[3] In its reports, MDRC uses the generic term "unpaid work experience" to describe CWEP and similar programs.

more effective when combined with other activities and targeted on participants specifically in need of work experience.

In MDRC's research, the cost to administering agencies of operating unpaid work experience ranged, in 1993 dollars, from $700 to $2,100 *per participant*. The *annual* cost of keeping one work experience slot filled ranged from $700 to $8,200, with the lowest costs found in the larger programs. Major expenses included worksite development; client intake, assignment and monitoring; and supportive services such as child care. In most, but not all, cases looked at by MDRC, the value to taxpayers of the program's output exceeded the program's cost. However, as cited above, participation in unpaid work experience appeared to have little net impact on the economic well-being of welfare recipients.

FOR ADDITIONAL READING

Brock, Thomas, David Butler and David Long. *Unpaid Work Experience for Welfare Recipients: Findings and Lessons from MDRC Research*. Manpower Demonstration Research Corporation. New York, Sept. 1993. 92 p.

Cook, Robert F., Charles F. Adams, Jr., and V. Lane Rawlins. *Public Service Employment: The Experience of a Decade*. W. E. Upjohn Institute for Employment Research, Kalamazoo, Michigan, 1985. 131 p.

Final Report on the WPA Program, 1935-43. Dec. 1946. 145 p.

Gueron, Judith M., and Edward Pauly. *From Welfare to Work*. Russell Sage Foundation, New York, 1991. 316 p.

Legislative Reference Service. *Civilian Conservation Corps*. Senate Document No. 215, 1962. 149 p.

Mirengoff, William, Lester Rindler, Harry Greenspan, Scott Seablom, and Lois Black. *The New CETA: Effect on Public Service Employment Programs*. National Research Council, Washington, 1980. 185 p.

Mirengoff, William, Lester Rindler, Harry Greenspan, and Charles Harris. *CETA: Accomplishments, Problems, Solutions*. Bureau of Social Science Research, Washington, Nov. 1981. 330 p.

Nathan, Richard P., Robert F. Cook, and V. Lane Rawlins. *Public Service Employment: A Field Evaluation*. Brookings Institution, Washington, 1981. 121 p.

Salmond, John A. *The Civilian Conservation Corps, 1933-1942: A New Deal Case Study*. Duke University Press, Durham, 1967. 240 p.

THE JOB TRAINING PARTNERSHIP ACT: A COMPENDIUM OF PROGRAMS

Molly R. Forman and Ann M. Lordeman

SUMMARY

The Job Training Partnership Act (JTPA), first enacted in 1982, is the country's chief employment training legislation. JTPA is composed of 15 programs and several national activities such as research an devaluation. The 15 programs primarily focus on the training needs of low income individuals facing significant barriers to employment. JTPA programs are frequently referred to as "second chance" program because they are intended to train persons who have not sufficiently benefited from traditional secondary and post-secondary education. All JTPA programs are funded through the Department of Labor (DOL). This report is intended to serve as a basic guide to the JTPA programs.

Funding for JTPA programs totals $5.4 billion on FY1995. Nearly three-quarters of this amount was appropriated for the four State and locally administered programs. Three of these provide training and employment services to low income adults and youths under Title Ii of the Act - the Adult Training program, the Summer Youth Employment and Training program, and the Youth Training program. The fourth, the Economic Dislocation and Worker Adjustment Assistance program, provided employment training assistance to permanently laid-off workers (i.e., dislocated workers) under Title III. These programs all have permanent authority and never need formal extension. Funds for these programs are allocated to States on the basis of a formula. All or part of the State's allocation is then sub-allocated to local entities according to the same or a similar formula.

Most of the delivery of services under JTPA's Title II and Ii programs take place at the local level. Each State is divided by the Governor into geographic areas referred to as service delivery areas (SDAs). Each SDA has a Private Industry Council (PIC) which provides policy guidance and oversight of it JTPA activities within the SDA. the majority of PIC members are representatives of the private sector.

Other JTPA programs are federally administered and include such programs as Job Corps, a residential program for severely disadvantaged youth; and programs for special population groups such as Native Americans, migrant and seasonal farmworkers, veterans, and young people living in high poverty areas (Youth Fair Chance). Federally administered programs account for approximately one quarter of JTPA's FY1995 appropriation. Job Corps is by far the largest of these programs.

INTRODUCTION

The Job Training Partnership Act is generally considered to be the country's major job training statute. Often mistakenly thought of as one program, JTPA actually authorizes 15 programs, and certain national activities, such as research, demonstration and pilot projects, evaluations, and training and technical assistance. Total FY1995 funding for JTPA programs and activities is $5.4 billion. Funds have been appropriated for 10 programs for FY1995.

This report is intended to serve as a basic reference guide to the 15 programs authorized by JTPA. The following section provides an overview of JTPA. Other sections provide detailed information on each of the programs, including a description of the services provided, eligibility requirements, and FY1995 funding level.

OVERVIEW

COMMON PROGRAM FEATURES

While JTPA programs vary in who they serve, the specific services they provide, and how they are administered, they do have several features in common:

- All programs are **funded through the Department of Labor** (DOL), and are subject to its regulations and policies.

- All programs **have a common goal**: to prepare youth and adults for participation in the labor force. JTPA programs are frequently referred to as "second chance " programs because they are intended to train persons who have not sufficiently benefited from traditional secondary and post-secondary education.

- All programs are **open to citizens, immigrants, refugees,** and other individuals authorized t work in the Untied States who meet the eligibility criteria. The programs are not open to undocumented aliens.

- **Participation in all programs ins voluntary**. There are no requirements that any individual enroll in training. This voluntary aspect of JTPA distinguishes it from some other job training programs, such as the Food Stamp training program, the Job Opportunities and Basic Skills (JOBS) program, and the Trade Adjustment Assistance programs. Under each of these programs, individuals meeting certain criteria are required to enroll in a training program in order to receive specific benefits, i.e., food stamps, Aid to Families with Dependent Children (AFDC) benefits, or trade readjustment allowances.

- **JTPA programs operate on a July through June program year**. In most cases, appropriations made in one fiscal year are for the upcoming JTPA program year.

RECIPIENTS OF SERVICES

In general, **JTPA programs are targeted to the poor**. In FY1995, nearly 75% of the funds appropriated are for programs that primarily serve low income persons. The eligibility requirements for some programs specify that individuals receiving services be **"economically disadvantaged."** This term as defined in statute and as used in this report, means that individuals or their families receive welfare payments or have a total family income that is not higher than the poverty line or 70% of the lower living standard income level.[1] Other persons who are considered economically disadvantaged are persons eligible for food stamps, homeless persons, disabled adults whose own income rather than their family income is low, and foster children whose care is subsidized by State or local governments.

Slightly more than half of all JTPA funds appropriated in FY1995 are for programs that serve low income youth or young adults primarily through three programs: the Summer Youth Employment and Training program, the Youth Training program (a year round program), and Job Corps (a primarily residential program). **Slightly less than half of the funds appropriated in FY1995 are for programs that serve adults age 22 and older** primarily through two programs: the Adult Training program for economically disadvantaged persons, and the Economic Dislocation and Worker Adjustment Assistance (EDWAA) program for permanently laid-off workers, who are not necessarily low income.

PROGRAM ADMINISTRATION

JTPA's programs can be grouped into two categories: (1) those administered directly by DOL, and (2) those administered by State and local entities. Programs directly administered by DOL are generally targeted to special population groups such as veterans, migrant and seasonal farmworkers, native Americans, young people needing intensive services provided in a residential setting (Job Corps), and young people living in high poverty areas (Youth Fair Chance). Federally administered programs account for approximately one quarter of JTPA's FY1995 appropriation. Job Corps is by far the largest federally administered program.

Programs administered by States and local entities are targeted to economically disadvantaged adults and youth and to permanently laid off workers (i.e., dislocated workers). Four programs are specifically State and locally administered: (1) the Adult Training program (Title II-A), (2) the Summer Youth Employment and Training program (Title II-B), (3) the Youth Training program (Tittle II-C), and (4) the Economic Dislocation Worker Adjustment Assistance (EDWAA) program (Title III). State and locally administered programs account for nearly three quarters of JTPA's FY1995 appropriation.

STRUCTURE OF STATE AND LOCALLY ADMINISTERED PROGRAMS

Most of the delivery of services under JTPA's Title II and II programs takes place at the local level. Each State is divided by the Governor into geographic areas referred to as service delivery areas (SDAs)[2] under Title II and as substate area (SSAs) under Title III.

---

[1] For 1994, the povery inocme guideline is $14,800 for a family of 4 except in Alaska and Hawaii where it is higher. The lower living standard income level (LLISL) is established by DOL for metropolitan and non-metropolitan areas in four major U.S. regions and in Alaska, Hawaii, and Guam; as well as 25 selected Metropolitan Statistical Areas. For a family of 4, 70% of the LLSIL (in the four regions) ranges from $14,760 in the non-metropolitan South to $17,880 in the metropolitan Northeast.

[2] A service delivery area is comprisd of the State or one or more units of gneral local government. A "unit of gneral local goverment" is any genral purpose political subdvision of a State which has the power to levy taxes and spend funds, as well as gneral corporate and police powers. The Governor must approve a request to be an SDA from (1) any unit of general local government with a population of 200,000 or more; (2) any consorita of contiguous units with an aggregate populatin of 200,000 or more, which serves a substantial part of one or more

(SSAs are composed of one or more SDAs with a total population of at least 200,000.) Each of the over 600 SDAs has a Private Industry Council (IC) which provides policy guidance and oversight for the JTPA activities within the SDA. PIC membership consists of representatives of :

- the private sector (majority of the PIC's membership),
- organized labor and community-based organizations[3] (at least 15% of the PIC's membership),
- educational agencies,
- vocational rehabilitation agencies,
- public assistance agencies,
- economic development agencies, and
- the public employment service.

Private sector members are to be business owners, chief executives of chief operating officers of nongovernmental employers, or other private sector executives who have substantial management of policy responsibility. Members are to reasonably represent the industrial and demographic composition of the business community; whenever possible, at least one half of the private sector members are to representatives of small business, including minority business. The chair of the PIC is to be a representative of the private sector.

For the Title II programs, the PIC and local elected officials must select a grant recipient to receive JTPA funds and an administrative entity responsible for the operation of the programs. These may be an administrative entity responsible for the operation of the programs. These may be separate entities, and can be: (1) the PIC, (2) a unit of general local government (or agency thereof), (3) a non-profit organization or corporation, or (4) any other agreed upon entity. The administrative entity may provide services directly or may select service providers. The PIC, in conjunction with local elected officials, also has responsibility for developing a 2-year job training plan, which details how JTPA activities will be carried out within the SDA. The plan must be approved by the Governor.

For the Title III EDWAA program, the Governor, the local elected officials and the PICs in the SSA select a grantee to be responsible for delivering services. the grantee may be: (1) a PIC, (2) an SDA grant recipient or administrative entity, (3) a private non-profit organization, (4) a unit of general local government (or agency thereof), (5) a local office of a State agency, or (6) another public agency, such as a community college or area vocational school. The substate grantee must develop a plan which details how JTPA activities will be carried out within the SSA. The plan must be approved by the Governor.

---

labor market areas; and (3) any concentrated employemtn program grantee for a rural area, which serve3d as a prime sponsor under the Comprehensive Employemtn and Training act (the predecessor to JTPA). The Governor may approve a request to be a SDA form a unit or consortia of unites of genral local governmetn with a population oless than 200,000, which serves a substantial protion of a labor mrket area.

[3] Community-based organizatins are nnprofit organizatins representaitve of communites or significant segments of communities which provide job training services, and organizations serving nonreservatio Indians, as well as tribal governments and Native Alaskan groups.

In addition to dividing the State into SDAs and SSAs and approving local plans for delivering services, the Governor also has a broad range of responsibilities including preparing the biennial Governor's Coordination and Special Services Plan (GCSSP),[4] administering statewide programs, implementing performance standards, establishing fiscal controls and fund accounting procedures, and establishing procurement standards and monitoring compliance with them.

Each State has a State Job Training Coordinating Council (SJTCC), which plans, coordinates and monitors the provision of programs and services. The Council does not operate programs or provide services. The SJTCC is composed as follows:

- 30% are representatives of business and industry;

- 30% are representatives of the State legislature, State agencies and organizations, units or consortia of general local government, and local educational agencies:

- 30% are representatives of organized labor and community-based organizations; and

- 10% are from the general public.

Either in addition to the SJTCC or as a replacement to it, the State can establish a State Human Resource Investment Council (HRIC) to advise the Governor on how to coordinate services and funds of federally funded human resource programs. The HRIC can replace the existing State councils of the program that agree to come under HRIC jurisdiction. These programs could include those authorized by JTPA, the Carl D. Perkins Vocational and Applied Technology Education Act,[5] the National and Community Services Act, the Adult Education Act, the Wagner-Peyser Act which authorizes the Employment Service, Part F of Title IV of the Social Security Act which authorizes the JOBS program, and the Food Stamp Act which authorizes a training program of food stamp recipients.

The HRIC is composed as follows:

- the head of each State agency responsible for the administration of an applicable Federal human resource program;

- at lest 15% are representatives of one or more of the following: local public education, a post secondary institution, a community-based organization (serving for a minimum of 2 years);

- at least 15% are representatives of business and industry (serving for a minimum of 2 years); and

- at least 15% are representatives of organized labor (serving for a minimum of 2 years).

---

[4] The GCSSP is a 2-year plain describing how the resources provided under JTPA will be used within the State and services delivery areas and evaluatin the experience of the previous 2 years. Included in the plan must be criteria for coordinating acitivies under this Act with related acitivies in the State. In addition to this plan, the Governor also submits a State plain developed on a biennial basis detailing the activities to be carried out under Title III. Both plans are submitted to the Secretary of Labor for approval.

[5] Any program authorized under the Perkins Act could be included under the jurisdiciton of th eHRIC only with the additional approval of the State Vocational Education Council.

Additional members may be representatives for local welfare agencies, public housing agencies, units or of consortia of units of general local government, the State legislature, any State of local program that receives funding under an applicable Federal human resource program, and individuals who have special knowledge and qualifications with respect to special education and career development of hard-to-serve individuals.

OTHER EMPLOYMENT AND TRAINING PROGRAMS

While JTPA programs are generally considered to be the country's major job training programs, other programs also provided job training. Indeed, one frequent criticism of Federal employment and training programs is that they are not coordinated with one another, resulting in a fragmented approach to employment and training rather than in a coordinated employment and training system. The General Accounting Office (GAO) estimates that in FY1993 there were more than 150 Federal employment and training programs in 14 agencies.[6] Most of these programs are quite small and narrowly focused, but any observers assert that they contribute to a piecemeal approach to job training ad lead to duplication of services and unnecessary administrative costs. Others assert that a wide range of categorical programs is needed to ensure that particular populations are served. One approach often recommended to create a more coherent Federal system is better coordination of programs. Three types of activities are often cited as including programs that could be better coordinated with JTPA programs:

Training to individuals provided by:

- State grants under the Vocational Rehabilitation Act;
- State grants under the Carl D. Perkins Vocational and Applied Technology Education Act;
- State programs under the Adult Education Act;
- The JOBS program under Part F of Title IV of the Social Security Act;
- The Food Stamp Employment and Training Program under the Food Stamp Act;
- Trade Adjustment Assistance under the Trade Act of 1974; and
- North American Free Trade Agreement (NAFTA) Transitional Assistance under the Trade Act of 1974.

Grants or loans to individuals for postsecondary training provided by:

- Pell Grants under the Higher Education Act, and
- Federal Family Education Loans also under the Higher Education Act.

---

[6] U.S. General Acconting Office. Testimony before the Senate Committee on Appropriatins. Subcommitte on Labor, Health and Human Services, and Education. June 1993; Multiple Employmetn Training Programs: Conflicting Requirements Hamper Delivery of Services (GAO/HEHS-94-78). Washington, Jan. 1994.

Labor exchange endeavors for employers seeking workers and workers seeking jobs provided by:

- the Employment Service under the Wagner-Peyser Act.

For information on these programs, see appendix E.

TRAINING SERVICES FOR THE DISADVANTAGED (TITLE II)

ADULT TRAINING PROGRAM

Authorization. Title II-A, JTPA as amended; permanently authorized.[7]

Services. The Adult Training Program provides direct training and training-related and supportive services to help prepare economically disadvantaged adults for participation in the workforce. The program requires an assessment of skills and service needs for each participant, the development of a service strategy to determine employment and achievement goals and appropriate services, and a review of participant progress.

Direct training services may include:

- basic skills training including remedial education, literacy training, and English-as-a-second-language training;
- on-the-job training;
- work experience;
- classroom training;
- programs to develop work habits;
- education-to-work transition actives;
- skill upgrading and retraining;
- entrepreneurial training; and
- job and career counseling.

Training-related and supportive services may include:

- job search assistance;
- outreach;
- supportive services such as transportation and child care;
- financial assistance; and
- follow-up services.

---

[7] P.L. 102-367, amending JTPA, was signed into law Sept. 7, 1992. The amendments created a new Title II-C to provide year-round services to economically disadvantaged youth. Title Ii-A, which previously served both adults and youth, will continue to serve economically disadvantaged adults, age 22 and older. These changes became effective on July 1, 1993, the beginning of program year 1993.

Service Delivery. The administrative enmity in the SDA can either provide services directly or through contracts with a variety of for-profit and non-profit service providers including schools and community colleges.

Eligibility and Targeting. Individuals 22 years of age and older who are economically disadvantage are eligible for the adult training program.[8] AT least 65% of participants must be in one or more of the following hard-to-serve categories:

- basic skills deficient;
- school dropouts;
- recipients of cash welfare payments (including recipients under the JOBS programs);
- offenders;
- disabled; and
- homeless

SDAs may add one additional category of hard-to-serve individuals, if approved by the Governor, and note solely comprised of individuals with a poor work history or who are unemployed.

Funding. Such sums as may be necessary are authorized to carry out Parts A and C (adult and youth training programs) of JTPA Title II. Not less than 40% of the total sum appropriated for Titles II-A and Ii-C must be provided to fund the Title II-A adult training program. $1,054.8 million was appropriated in FY1995. No matching funds are required except for a limited amount of State funds set aside for education coordination activities (see below).

As shown in Figure 1, the DOL allocates funds to the States according t a three-part formula based equally on the relative number of unemployed individuals living in areas with high jobless rates, the relative excess number of unemployed individuals, and the relative number of economically disadvantaged adults.

States allocate 77% of their allotment to SDAs using the same three-part formula. (An SDA may transfer up to 10% of its allocation to the youth training programs (II-C), if the transfer is described in the job training plan submitted to and approved by the Governor.) SDAs must spend at least 50% of their allocation on direct training services and not more than 20% on administration. The balance of the SDA allocation is for training-related and supportive services.

Twenty-three percent of the State allotment is set aside for statewide activities: 5 percent for administration; 5% for incentive grants to SDAs for exceeding performance standards; 8% for education grants (see below); and 5% for services to adults 55 years of age and older (see below).

Participation (DOL est.). Program Year 1994: 433,500.

State education coordination and grants. State are required to use 8% of their Title II-A funds for programs to provide school-to-work transition services; literacy and life-long learning opportunities and services; a statewide approach to train, place, and retain women in non-traditional employment; and coordination of programs and services.

---

[8] Up to 10% of participants need not be economicaly disadvantaged provided that they face one or more serious barriers to employemtn. Serious barriers to employment include the hard-to-serve categories listed above and other such as displaced homemakers, veterans, alcohlics, and drug addicts.

Program funds must be used primarily to service economically disadvantaged individuals. Some dislocated workers and persons with barriers to employment who are not economically disadvantaged may also be served. All Federal funds must be equally matched by the States.

Services for older individuals (older worker set-aside). States are required to use 5% of their Title Ii-A funds for programs to train and place older individuals in employment opportunities in the private sector. Persons 55 years of age and older who are economically disadvantaged are eligible for services.[9] Services are provided by public agencies, private nonprofit businesses, PICs, and SDAs.

SUMMER YOUTH EMPLOYMENT AND TRAINING PROGRAM

Authorization. Title II-B, JTPA as amended; permanently authorized.
Services. The Summer Youth Employment and Training program provides employment and training activities during the summer months for economically disadvantaged youths to strengthen basic educational skills, encourage school completion, provide work exposure, and enhance citizenship skills. The program requires an assessment of skills and service needs for each participant, the development of a service strategy to determine employment and achievement goals and appropriate services, and a review of participant progress. Services may include:

- basic and remedial education;
- academic enrichment;
- institutional and on-the-job training;
- work experience in public and private nonprofit organizations, which to the extent feasible integrates the development of general competencies with the development of academic skills;
- classroom training, which to extent feasible, includes opportunities to apply academic knowledge and skills to the world of work;
- occupational training;
- employment counseling;
- job search assistance and job club activities; and
- supportive services such as transportation.

Young people generally receive wages for participation in the program,. Those who have been assessed as needing basic ad remedial education or preemployment and work maturity skills training must be provided them either directly by the program or through arrangements with other programs.

Service Delivery. The administrative entity in the SDA can either provide services directly or through contracts with a variety of for-profit and non-profit service providers including schools and community colleges.

---

[9] Up to 10% of particpants need not be eonomically disadvantaged provided that they face serious barriers to employment and meet income eligibility requirements for th eolder worker employment program authorized by Title V of the Older Americans Act (135% of poverty).

Eligibility and Targeting. Youths aged 14-21 who are economically disadvantaged or eligible for free meals under the school lunch program are eligible for the program. Participants may be concurrently enrolled in both the Summer Youth program and the year-round Youth Training program (II-C).

Funding. Such sums as may be necessary are authorized to carry out Title II-B. $1,056.3 million was appropriated in FY 1995. The Summer Youth Employment and Training program is entirely federally funded. No matching funds are required. Fiscal year appropriations for Summer Youth are generally spent at the end of a program year, that is, the summer of the following calendar year. FY1990 appropriations, for example, were spent in the summer of 1991. However, as shown in table 1 below, Summer Youth appropriations have, in recent fiscal years, included amounts to be spent in more than one summer.

Table 1. Funding Availability for the Summer Youth Employment and Training Program, FY1992-FY1995 ($ in millions)

	FY1992 approp.	FY1993 approp.	FY1994 approp.	FY1995 approp.	Amount available
For use in summer 1992	$500.00				$1,182.9
For use in summer 1993	495.2	$354.2			849.4
For use in summer 1994		670.7	$206.0		876.7
For use in summer 1995			682.3	$184.8	867.1
For use in summer 1996				871.5	971.5

Includes $682.9 million appropriated in FY1991 for summer 1992.

As shown in figure 1, DOL allocates funds to the States according to a three-part formula based equally on the relative number of unemployed individuals living in areas with high jobless rates, the relative excess number of unemployed individuals, and the relative number of economically disadvantaged youth.

States allocate their total allotment to SDAs using the same three-part formula based equally on the relative number of unemployed individuals living in areas with high jobless rates, the relative excess number of unemployed individuals and the relative number of economically disadvantaged youth.

States allocate their total allotment to SDAs using the same three-part formula. (An SDA may transfer up to 20% of summer youth program funds to the youth training program (II-C) if approved by the Governor.) Not more than 15% of funds may be spent on administration.

Participation (DOL est.). Program Year 1994 (Summer 1995): 623,000.

YOUTH TRAINING PROGRAM

Authorization. Title II-C of the JTPA as amended; permanently authorized.[10]

Services. The Youth Training Program provides direct training and training-related and supportive services to help prepare economically disadvantaged youths for participation in the workforce. The program request an assessment of skills and service needs for each participant, the development of a service strategy to determine employment and achievement goals and appropriate services, and a review of participant progress. Direct training may include:

- basic skills training including remedial education, literacy training, and English-as-a-second-language training;
- on-the-job training;
- job and career counseling;
- work experience;
- tutoring and study skills training;
- instruction leading to high school completion or the equivalent;
- school-to-work transition services; and
- preemployment and work maturity skills training.

Training-related and supportive services may include:

- job search assistance;
- supportive services such as transportation and child care;
- drug and alcohol abuse counseling;
- services to encourage involvement of parents, spouses, and other significant adults; and
- cash incentives based on attendance and performance in a program.

Service Delivery. the administrative entity in the SDA can either provide services directly or thorough contracts with a variety of for-profit and non-profit service providers including schools and community colleges.

Eligibility and Targeting. In-school youths, age 16-21 (or 14-21 in some cases) are eligible for participation if they are economically disadvantaged,[11] participating in a Chapter 1 compensatory education program under the Elementary and Secondary Education Act, or eligible for a free meal under the National School Lunch Act during the most recent school year. Youths not in school, ages 16-21, are eligible if economically

---

[10] P.L. 102-367, amending JTPA, was singed into law Sept. 7, 1992. The amendments created a new Title II-C to provide year-round services to economically disadvantaged youth. Title II-A prviously provided services for eonomically disadvantaged adults and youth. (Local SDAs receiving Ii-A funds were requreied to spend at least 40% of their funds on eligile youth, ages 16-21). Title II-A will continue to service economically disadvantaged adults, age 22 nad older. These changes became effective on July 1, 1993, the beginning of prgram year 1993.

[11] Up to 10% of particpants need not be economically disadvantaged provided that they face one or more serious barriers to employment. Serious barriers to employment include the hard-to-serve categories listed above and others such as sindividuals with limited English proficiency, alcholocsm, and drug addicts.

disadvantaged. At least 50% of participants in each SDA must be out of school. At least 65% of youths in each group must be in one or more of the following hard-to-serve categories.

- basic skills deficient;
- in a grade below their age appropriate grade level (if in-school);
- school dropouts (if out-of-school);
- pregnant or parenting;
- disable, including learning disabled;
- homeless or run-away youth; and
- offenders.

SDAs may add one additional category of hard-to-serve individuals, if approved by the Governor, and not solely comprised of individuals with a poor work history or who are unemployed.

All youths are eligible to participate in school-wide projects, regardless of income if enrolled in a public school that meets the following criteria:

- located in a poverty area;[12]
- served by a local educational agency eligible for assistance under Chapter 1 of the Elementary and Secondary Education Act;
- at least 70% of the students are considered hard-to-serve; and
- conducts a program under a cooperative agreement between the SDA and the local educational agency.

Funding. Such sums as may be necessary are authorized to carry out Parts A and C (Adult and Youth Training programs) of JTPA Title II. Not less than 40% of the total sum appropriated for Titles II-A and II-C must be provided to fund the Title II-C youth training program; %598.7 million was appropriated in FY1995. No matching funds are required except for a limited amount of State funds set aside for education coordination activities (see below).

As shown in figure 1, the DOL allocates funds to the States according to a three-part formulas based equally on the relative number of unemployed individuals living in areas with high jobless rates, the relative excess number of unemployed individuals, and the relative number of economically disadvantaged youth.

States allocate 82% of their allotment to service delivery areas using the same three-part formula. (An SDA may transfer up to 10% of its allocation to the adult training program (II-A), if the transfer is described in the job training plan submitted to and approved by the Governor.) SDAs must spend at least 50% of their allocation on direct training services and not more than 20% n administration. The balance of the SDA allocation is for training-related and supportive services.

---

[12] Defind here, by law, as an urban census tract or a nonmetropolitan county with a poverty rate of 30% or more as defined by the Census Bureau.

The remaining 18% of the State allocation is set aside for statewide activities; 5% for administration; 5% for incentive grants to SDAs for exceeding performance standards; and 8% for education grants (see below).

Participation (DOL est.). Program Year 1994: 348,400.

State education coordination and grants. States are required to use 8% of their Title II-C funds for programs to provide school-to-work transition services; literacy and life-long learning opportunities and services; a statewide approach to train, place and retail women in non-traditional employment and coordination of programs and services. Program funds must be used primarily to serve economically disadvantaged individuals. Some dislocated workers and persons with barriers to employment may also be served. All Federal funds must be equally matched by the States.

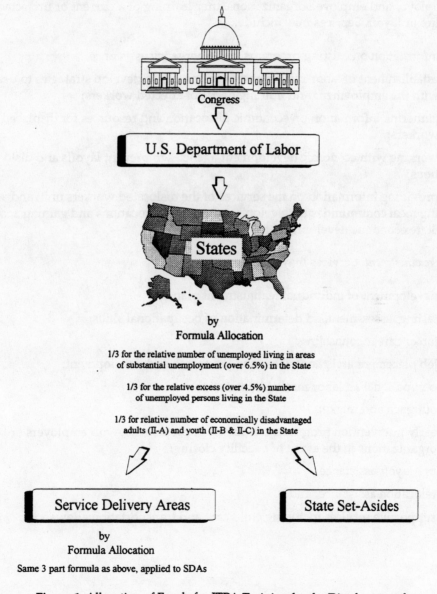

Figure 1. Allocation of Funds for JTPA Training for the Disadvantaged

EMPLOYMENT AND TRAINING ASSISTANCE
FOR DISLOCATED WORKERS (TITLE III)

ECONOMIC DISLOCATION AND WORKER ADJUSTMENT ASSISTANCE (EDWAA) PROGRAM

Authorization. Title III, JTPA as amended; permanently authorized.
Services. The EDWAA program provides training and training-related services to assist workers in obtaining jobs, regardless of the cause of their dislocation. Services may be broken down into four categories.

1) *Rapid response.* Specialists in the Sate dislocated worker unit make immediate contact with employer and employee organizations after learning of a current or projected facility closure or layoff. Services may include.

- information on existing programs and emergency assistance;
- establishment of labor-management committees to develop strategies to deal with the employment and training needs of affected workers;
- gathering information on economic dislocation and resources for displaced workers;
- working with economic development agencies to prevent layoffs and dislocations;
- providing information on the services of the dislocated workers unit; and assisting local communities to develop responses to dislocations and gaining access to State economic development assistance.

2) *Basic readjustment.* Services may include:

- development of individual readjustment plans;
- testing, assessment, ad determination of occupational skills;
- job or career counseling;
- job placement assistance, job clubs, job search and development;
- occupational ad labor market information;
- outreach and intake;
- early intervention programs conducted in cooperation with employers or labor organizations in the event of a facility closing;
- pre-layoff assistance;
- relocation assistance; and
- supportive services including child care and transportation allowances.

3) *Retraining*. Services may include:

- classroom training;
- occupational skill training;
- on-job-training;
- entrepreneurial training;
- basic and remedial education including literacy training and English-as-a-second-language;
- out-of-area job search; and
- relocation.

4) *Income Support*. Cash payments may be provided to participants who do not qualify for unemployment compensation or have exhausted their benefits and need income support in order to participate in the program.

Service Delivery. Each State designates or creates an identifiable dislocated worker unit to provide "rapid response" actives. The State cannot transfer the responsibility of providing these services to another entity, but can contract for them with another entity. The substate grantee may provide basic readjustment services, retraining, and income support directly or through contract, grant, or agreement with service providers.

Eligibility and Targeting. Workers eligible for services under EDWAA are:

- persons who have lost their job or received notice of termination, are eligible for unemployment compensation or have exhausted their benefits, and are unlikely to return to their previous work;

- persons who have been terminated or have received notice of termination as a result of a permanent closing or substantial layoff;

- persons who are long-term unemployed with limited opportunities for employment in a similar occupation in their area of residence, including older workers whose age creates a barrier to employment; and

- persons who were self-employed, including farmers and ranchers, unemployed as a result of general economic conditions or natural disasters.[13]

Most *basic* readjustment services become available upon public announcement of a facility closing. All services become available 180 days before a scheduled closing, whether the worker has received specific notice or not.

Funding. such sums as may be necessary are authorized. $1,296.0 million was appropriated for FY1995. The program is entirely federally funded.

Eighty percent of funds appropriated for EDWAA goes to a State "formula" grant program. As shown in figure 2, the DOL allocates funds to the States according to a three part formula based equally on the relative number of unemployed, the relative number of excess unemployed, and the relative number of long-term unemployed, Governors may reserve up to 40% of this state allocation for State level activities. Another 10% can be reserved for distribution during the first 9 months of the program year to

---

[13] In addition, displaced homemakers may receive services of the Governor determines that they can be served without adversely affecting services to other dislocated workers.

local areas with unforeseen need. At least 50% of a State's allocation must be passed to substate areas by a State formula.

States and substate grantees may generally use their discretion in deciding which authorized services to fund and how much to spend on them. There are, however, some limitations. Not less than half of funds allocated to a substate grantee must be spent on retaining, unless the grantee has obtained a waiver from the Governor. (Waivers allow grantees to spend less than 50% but more than 30%). Not more than 25 % of funds allocated to a substate grantee or to the Governor may be spent on needs-related payments and supportive services; not more than 15% may be spent on administration.[14]

Twenty percent of funds appropriated for EDWAA is reserved by the Secretary of Labor for Federal responsibilities, including a discretionary grant program. Discretionary grants are available for a variety of dislocated worker projects including those that provide services needed as a result of mass layoffs caused by natural disasters or Federal actions.

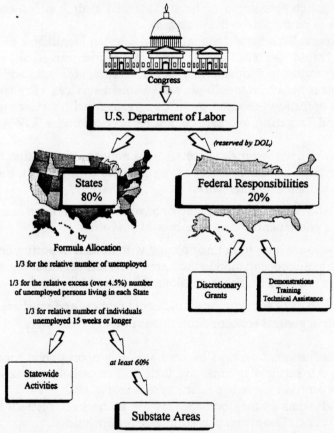

Figure 2. Allocation of Funds for JTPA Economic Dislocation and Worker Adjustment Assistance (EDWAA) Program (Title III)

---

[14] P.L. 103-33. FY1995 Appropriation Act ofr th eDepartments of Labor, Health and Human Serives, Education, and Related Agencies elimiantes cost limitations on needs-related paymetns and supportive services. It also modifies State waiver authirty to allow waivers to be granted if a substate grantee demonstrates to the Fovernor that it is appropriate due to the availability of low-cost traiing servies, to facilitate needs-related paymetns to accompany long-term training, or to facilitate appropriate basic readjustment services. These provisions apply to funds appropriated in P.L. 103-333 FY1995 funding).

DEFENSE CONVERSION ASSISTANCE PROGRAM (DCA)

Authorization. Title III, Sec. 325, JTPA, as amended; authorized through FY1997. DCA was added to JTPA by the National Defense Authorization Act for FY1991.

Services. DCA provides training and training-related services to assist workers dislocated by reductions in defense spending. Services that can be provided include the rapid response, basic readjustment, retraining, and income support services described under EDWAA.

Service Delivery. States, substate grantees, employers, employer associations, and representatives of employees may apply to the DOL for grants to provide services to eligible individuals.

Eligibility and Targeting. Persons eligible for services under the DCA program must meet the eligibility criteria for the EDWAA and have been laid off, terminated, or have received notice of layoff or termination due to reductions in defense spending, base closures, or reductions in the export of defense articles and services.

Funding. $150.0 million was appropriated in FY1991. These funds are available for obligation until Sept. 30, 1997. The Secretary may also make grants form funds reserved for Federal responsibilities under Title II (Secretary's reserve - 20% of EDWAA funds). Funds are available from the DOL through a grant application process.

Participation (OMB est.). Over 45,000 persons served as of March 31, 1994.

DEFENSE DIVERSIFICATION PROGRAM (DDP)

Authorization. Title III, Sec. 325A, JTPA, as amended; authorized for FY1993. The defense diversification program was added to JTPA by the National Defense Authorization Act for FY1993.

Services. DDP provides training and training-related services to assist certain members of the armed forces and some defense and defense contractor employees. Services that can be provided included the rapid response, basic readjustment, retraining, and income support services described under the EDWAA program. Funds may also be used to:

- provide skills upgrading for non-managerial employees;
- promote development of high performance workplace systems;
- encourage participative management systems; and
- further employee participation in evaluation, selection, and implementation of new production technologies.

Service Delivery. States, substate grantees, employers, representatives of employees, labor-management committees, and other employer-employee entities may apply to the DOL for grants to provide services to eligible individuals.

Eligibility and Targeting. Members of the armed services or National Guard, not entitled to retirement or retainer pay, are eligible for services if they were on active duty or employed full-time on Sept. 30, 1990, and are separated from duty involuntarily or through a separation program during the subsequent 5 years. Application must be made within 180 days of separation from duty.

Civilian employees of the Departments of Defense and Energy (DOD/DOE), not entitled to retirement or retainer pay, are eligible for services if they are terminated or laid off or have received notice of termination of layoff due to reductions in defense spending or closure or realignment of a military installation during the 5-year period beginning Oct. 1, 1992. Employees receiving notification of termination or layoff are eligible for services 180 days before the projected date of termination. Civilian DOD employees affected by a base closure or realignment can receive services up to 2 years before its completion.

Defense contractor employees, not entitled to retirement or retainer pay, are eligible for services if they are terminated or laid off or have received notice of termination or layoff due to reductions in defense spending, closure or realignment of a military installation, or reductions in the export of defense articles and services during the 5-year period beginning Oct. 1, 1992. (Contractors must have DOD contracts or subcontracts connected with a defense contract totaling at least $0.5 million.)

Funding. $75.0 million was appropriated by the National Defense Appropriations act, 1993. These funds were available for obligation until Sept. 30, 1994. The Secretary may make grants from funds reserved for Federal responsibilities under Title III (Secretary's reserve - 20% of EDWAA funds). Funds are available from DOL through a grant application process.

Participation (OMB est.). Over 2,000 persons served as of March 31, 1994.

CLEAN AIR EMPLOYMENT TRANSITION ASSISTANCE PROGRAM (CAETA)

Authorization. Title III, Sec. 326, JTPA as amended; authorized through FY1995. CAETA was aided to JTPA by the Clean Air Act Amendments of 1990.

Services. CAETA provides training and training-related services to assist workers dislocated as a result of compliance with the Clean Air Act. Services that can be provided include the rapid response, basic readjustment, retraining, and income support services described under the EDWAA program.

Service Delivery. States, substate grantees, employers, employer associations, and representatives of employees may apply to the DOL for grants to provide services to eligible individuals.

Eligibility and Targeting. Persons eligible for services under the CAETA program must meet the eligibility criteria for the EDWAA program and have been laid off or terminated or received notice of layoff or termination as a result of compliance with the Clean Air Act.

Funding. CAETA was authorized at $50.0 million for FY1991 and such sums as may be necessary for fiscal years 1992 through 1995. The total appropriation for the e 5 fiscal years cannot exceed $250.0 million. Appropriated funds are available until expended. Funds are available from DOL through a grant application process. No new funds were appropriated for FY1995. CAETA was last funded in FY1993 at $49.6 million.

Participation. Not available.

FEDERALLY ADMINISTERED PROGRAMS (TITLE IV)

NATIVE AMERICAN PROGRAMS

Authorization. Title IV-A, Sec. 401, JTPA as amended; permanently authorized.

Services. JTPA's Native American Programs are designed to support the growth and development of Native Americans and to improve their economic well being in a way consistent with the goals and lifestyles of their communities. The programs provide services to help participants gain permanent, unsubsidized employment. According to regulations, services may include:

- job training;

- work experience;

- counseling;

- job referral; and

- employment-related services including child care, transportation, and training allowances.

Service Delivery. Indian tribes and reservations, and other Native American groups provide services to eligible individuals.

Eligibility and Targeting. Indians, Eskimos, Aleuts, Native Hawaiians and other persons of Native American descent who are economically disadvantaged, unemployed, or underemployed are eligible for the program.

Funding. An amount equal to not more than 7% of JTPA's total appropriation is authorized to be appropriated for Parts A, C, D, E, F, and G of JTPA Title IV.[15] From this amount, an amount equal to not less than 3.3% of the total funding available for Title II-A and II-C is reserved for the Native American Programs. $64.1 million was appropriated in FY1995 (equal to 3.9% of II-A plus II-C).

The DOL allocates funds to grantees using a formula based on poverty and unemployment rates among Native Americans. Approximately 185 formula grants are issued each year.

Participation (DOL est.). Program Year 1994: 29,410 participants.

MIGRANT AND SEASONAL FARMWORKER PROGRAMS

Authorization. Title IV-A, Sec. 402, JTPA as amended; permanently authorized.

Services. The Migrant and Seasonal Farmworker Programs are designed to help farmworkers obtain or retain secure, stable employment at an income above the poverty level, and to improve the standard of living of workers remaining in the agricultural market. The programs provide training and other employment related services, which according to regulations, may include:

- job search assistance;

- classroom training;

- on-the-job training;

- work experience; and

- supportive services including transportation, personal and financial counseling, health care, child care, temporary shelter, meals, and legal assistance.

---

[15] Employment and Training Programs for Native Americans and Migrant and Seasonal Farmworkers, Veterans' Employment Programs, National Activities, Labor market Information, National Commission for Employment Policy, and Training to Fulfull Affirmative Action Obligations.

Service Delivery. Public agencies and nonprofit organizations provide services to eligible individuals.

Eligibility and Targeting. According to regulations, eligibility for this program is limited to migrant or seasonal farmworkers and their dependents who have

- earned more than half of their income through farmwork or been employed as a farmworker for at least half of the time during a consecutive 12 month period within the preceding 24 months; and

- whose family receives public assistance or whose family income does not exceed the higher of either the poverty level of 70% of the DOL's lower living standard income level.

Funding. An amount equal to not more than 7% of JTPA's total appropriation is authorized to be appropriated for Parts A, C, D, E, F, and G of JTPA Title IV.[16] From this amount, an amount equal to not less than 3.2 % of the total funding available for Title II-A and II-C is reserved for the Migrant and Seasonal Farmworker Programs. $85.7 million was appropriated in FY1995 (equal to 5.2% of II-A plus II-C).

Up to 6% of funds allotted to the programs may be set aside for a national account for technical assistance and special projects. At least 94% of the funds are to be allocated for grants to programs in individual States. The amount of the grants is determined by a formulas based on the best available data on farmworker population.

Participation (DOL est.). Program Year 1994: 64,100 participants.

JOB CORPS

Authorization. Title IV-B, JTPA as amended; permanently authorized.

Services. Job Corps is a residential employment and training program[17] to assist economically disadvantaged youths who need and can benefit from an unusually intensive program operated in a group environment. Services include:

- intensive remedial education including reading, mathematics, and preparation for the high school equivalency examination (GED);

- vocational training;

- social skills training;

- work experience;

- counseling;

- health care, day care, substance abuse programs, and other supportive services; and

- meals, lodging, clothing and personal (incentive-based allowances, an d recreational programs.

---

[16] Employment and Training Programs for Native Americans and Migrant and Seasonal Farmworkers, Veterans' employment Programs, National Activities, Labor Market Information, National Commission for Employment Policy, and Training to Fulfill Affirmative Action Obligations.

[17] Up to 20% of enrollees may be nonresidential. Priority for nonresidential particpation is givn to single parents.

Enrollees may remain in Job Corps for up to 2 years. The average stay is about 8 months. Upon leaving Job Corps, placement assistance is provided to help students find a job, return to school, or enter the armed forces.

Service Delivery. There are 111 Job Corps Centers currently in operation. Eighty of the centers are operated by major corporations and nonprofit organizations under contract with the DOL. (The Federal Government provides the facilities and equipment.) The remaining centers, known as Civilian Conservation Corps Centers, are operated by the Departments of Agriculture and Interior on public lands and are staffed by Federal employees.

Eligibility and Targeting. Economically disadvantaged 14–24 year olds living in a highly disruptive environment who are free of serious medical or behavioral problems are eligible for Job Corps.[18]

Funding. Such sums as may be necessary are authorized to e appropriated for the Job Corps. $1,099.5 million was appropriated in FY1995.

Participation (DOL est.). Program Year 1994: Not available. There were 102,098 participants in Program Year 1993.

VETERANS' EMPLOYMENT PROGRAMS

Authorization. Title IV-C, JTPA as amended; permanently authorized.

Services. JTPA's Veterans Employment Programs develop and promote job and job training opportunities for eligible veterans, enhance employment and training services available from other providers, and furnish outreach and public information. According to regulations, services may include:

- counseling;
- vocational and aptitude testing;
- career assessment;
- remedial education; and
- job placement.

Service Delivery. The Secretary of Labor through the Assistant Secretary for Veterans' Employment and Training awards grants or contracts to public agencies and private and nonprofit organizations. Service delivery is coordinated with other JTPA programs, the U.S. Employment Service, and employment and training programs at the State and local level.

Eligibility. All service disabled veterans, Vietnam-era veterans, and veterans recently separated from military service are eligible for services.

Funding. An amount equal to not more than 7% of JTPA's total appropriation is authorized to be appropriated for Parts A, C, D, E, F, and G of JTPA Title IV.[19] Seven percent of the amount appropriated to these parts is reserved for Title IV-C, Veterans

---

[18] By law, 14 and 15 year olds are eligible to particpate in Job Corps. However, regualtions limit their enrollment to selected cases. In addition, the law permits up to 20% of enrollees to be 22-24 years old.

[19] Employment and Training Programs for Native Americans and Migrant and Seasonal Farworkers, Veterans' Employemtn Programs, Natinal Activities, Labor Market Inofrmation, National Commission for Employment Policy, and Training to Fulfill Affirmative Action Obligations.

Employment Programs. $8.9 million was appropriated in FY1995 (equal to 3.8% of IV-A, C, D, E, F, and G).

Not less than 80% of the funds is distributed to the States. Up to 20% of IV-C funds is reserved for training projects that are national in scope, pilot and research projects, and other activities to help train veterans for jobs.

Participation (DOL est.). Program Year 1994: Not available. 3.135 veterans have been served (under the 80% formula funds) as of Program Year 1993.

YOUTH FAIR CHANCE PROGRAM (YFC)

Authorization. Title IV-H, JTPA as amended; authorized through FY1997. The Youth Fair Chance Program was created by the Job Training Reform Amendments of 1992 (P.L. 102-367).

Services. The Youth Fair Chance Program awards grants to high poverty areas[20] in urban and rural communities to provide a comprehensive range of education, employment, and training services to all youths residing in the target community. A number of grant recipients will be permitted to establish job guarantee programs for eligible youths. Participating communities will be involved in determining what services are needed and who will provide them. DOL has recommended that YFC projects include separate components for in-school and out-of-school youth.[21]

Service Delivery. The Secretary of Labor is authorized to select up to 25 communities as grant recipients for the program's first fiscal year. Grants are awarded on a competitive basis to local SDAs. Designated Migrant and Seasonal Farmworker and Native American grantees are also eligible as grant recipients on behalf of their community. Sixteen grants were award in 1994. Grants will operate for 18 months initially with the possibility of continued funding.

Eligibility and Targeting. All youths and young adults, age 14030 at time of enrollment, in a selected community shall be eligible to participate, regardless of income. For the job guarantee program, all youths, age 16-19, residing in the area shall be eligible, regardless of income if they meet school attendance and performance standards and commit to completing high school.

Funding. $100.0 million is authorized to be appropriated for FY1993 and such sums as may be necessary for each succeeding fiscal year through FY1997 for Title IV-H, the Youth Fair Chance program. $24.8 million was appropriated in FY1995.

The Federal Government will provide at least 70% of the funds for the cost of this program. Grant recipients may meet up to 20% of the remaining costs with funds from other Federal sources, and must provide at least 10% from nonfederal sources or in-kind contribution. Not more than 5% of the funds appropriated are to be used for technical assistance, an independent evaluation, and a report to Congress.

Participation. Not available.

[20] Areas wihtin communities that have a poverty rate of at least 30%.
[21] 58 FR 67816.

MICROENTERPRISE GRANTS PROGRAM

Authorization. Title IV-I, JTPA as amended; authorized through 1997. The Microenterprise Grants Program was created by the Job Training Reform Amendments of 1992 (P.L. 102-367).

Services. The microenterprise grants program provides technical assistance, training, and counseling to help develop small commercial enterprises. A microenterprise is a commercial enterprise with five or fewer employees, one or more of whom is the owner. Owners must be economically disadvantaged. Grants will be awarded to implement and enhance community-based microenterprise activities, including the training of program staff,

Service Delivery. The Secretary of Labor is authorized to award up to 10 grants to States and designated Native American and Migrant and Seasonal Farmworker grantees to provide services. Grants are awarded on a competitive basis. Five grants were awarded in 1994. According to DOL, grant duration will be 15 months with the possibility of a 1-year extension.

Eligibility and Targeting. Economically disadvantaged owners of commercial enterprises with five or fewer employees, at least one of whom is the employer, are eligible for services under the program.

Funding. $5.0 million is authorized to be appropriated for each year FY1993-FY1997 for Title IV-I, the Microenterprises Grants Program. $2.2 million was appropriated in FY1995.

The Secretary will award grants of up to $0.5 million per year. Grantees must match all Federal funds with an equal amount of nonfederal cash or in-kind contributions.

Participation. Not available.

DISASTER RELIEF EMPLOYMENT ASSISTANCE

Authorization. Title IV-J, JTPA as amended; permanently authorized. The Disaster Relief Employment Assistance Program was created by the Job Training Reform Amendments of 1992 (P.L. 102-367).

Services. The Disaster Relief Employment Assistance Program provides employment for persons affected by an emergency or natural disaster. Employment will be on projects offering

- humanitarian assistance such as food, clothing, and shelter; and

- demolition, cleanup, repair, renovation, and reconstruction.

Employment is limited to 6 months of work related to recovery from a single natural disaster.

Service Delivery. Projects may be operated by units of local government and private and public agencies and organizations engaged in relief work.

Eligibility. Persons eligible for the Title III programs for dislocated workers, the Sec. 401 program for Native Americans, the Sec. 402 program for Migrant and Seasonal Farmworkers, and persons left unemployed as a result of the disaster are eligible for the Disaster Relief Employment Assistance Program.

Funding. $15.0 million is authorized to be appropriated for FY1993 and such sums as may be necessary for each succeeding fiscal year for Title IV-J, the Disaster Relief Employment Assistance Program. No funds have ever been appropriated.

If appropriated, funds would be made available by the Secretary of Labor to the Governor of any State within an area that has suffered an emergency or major disaster. Not less than 80% of these funds will be allocated by the Governor to units of local government in the affected area. The remaining funds may be reserved by the Governor for rescue, cleanup, and associated activities.

Participation. Not applicable. The program has never been funded.

JOBS FOR EMPLOYABLE DEPENDENT INDIVIDUALS (JEDI) INCENTIVE BONUS PROGRAM (TITLE V)

Authorization. Title V, JTPA as amended; authorized through 1996. JEDI was added to JTPA by the Stewart B. McKinney Homeless Assistance Amendments Act of 1988 (P.L. 100-628).

Program Description. JEDI pays bonuses to States for providing job training to certain individuals who have successfully participated in education, training, or other JTPA activities. These individuals are:

- absent parents of children receiving payments under AFDC who pay child support following training; and

- blind or disabled recipients of Supplemental Security Income (SSI) who earn a wage or income from unemployment after training.

Most of a bonus is to be used by the State for JTPA services to disadvantaged adults and youth and participants in Job Corps. Up to 5% may be used for administrative purposes at the State and local level.

Funding. Such sums as may be necessary are authorized to be appropriated through FY1996. Prior to the 1992 amendments, funds for JEDI could only be appropriated if funds for JTPA's Title II program for disadvantaged adults and youths exceeded the previous year's appropriation by an amount equal to or exceeding any increase in the consumer price index. This never occurred and funds for JEDI were never appropriated. The 1992 amendments removed this "trigger," but the program has still never received appropriations.

Participation. Not applicable. The program has never been funded.

APPENDIX A

Sections 1-4
Contain table of contents, statement of purpose, authorization of appropriations, and definitions.

Title I. JTPA Requirements
Authorizes, describes, and provides procedures for the State and local service delivery system; outlines Federal responsibilities.

Title II. Training Services for the Disadvantaged
Authorizes and describes training programs for economically disadvantaged adults (Part A) and youths (Part C) and summer employment and training programs for youth (Part B).

Title III. Employment and Training Assistance for Dislocated Workers
Authorizes and describes training programs for dislocated workers including the EDWAA program, the Defense Conversion Adjustment program (DCA), the Defense Diversification Program (DDP), and the Clean Air Employment Transition Assistance Program (CAETA).

Title IV. Federally Administered Programs
Authorizes employment and training programs for native Americans ad migrant and seasonal farmworkers (Part A) and veterans (Part C); Job Corps (Part B); National Activities (Part D) including technical assistance, research, demonstration and pilot programs; activities related to collection and availability of labor market information (Part E); National Commission for Employment Policy (Part F); activities related to raining and to fulfill affirmative action requirements (Part G); Youth Fair Chance (P[art H); Microenterprise Grants (Part I); and Disaster Relief Employment Assistance (Part J).

Title V. Jobs for Employable Dependent Individuals Incentive Bonus Program
Authorizes the payment of incentive bonuses to States for the successful job placement of absent parents of children receiving AFDC and to blind and disabled persons receiving SSI.

Title VI. Miscellaneous Provisions
Contains amendments to the Wagner-Peyser Act (U.S. Employment Service), provisions for an earning disregard of JTPA income earned by dependents in AFDC families, and policy of compliance with Military Selective Service Act. Authorizes and describes the State job bank system.

Title VII. State Human Resource Investment Council
Authorizes voluntary establishment of State Human Resource Investment Councils to advise Governors on coordination of services and funds or related programs.

APPENDIX B: BRIEF LEGISLATIVE HISTORY OF JTPA
29 U.S.C. 1501 ET SEQ.

Job Training Partnership Act (JTPA)
P.L. 97-300, signed October 13, 1982, 96 Stat. 1324
Established a major new federally funded employment and training system to replace
the Comprehensive Employment and Training Act of 1973 (CETA). Under JTPA, States
and localities become primarily responsible for administering the program; local representatives of the private sector play a key role in program planning an monitoring;
training for unsubsidized jobs is emphasized; and compliance with performance standards is required.

JTPA Amendments of 1986
P.L. 99-496, signed November 16, 1986, 100 State. 1261
Fine tuned the 1982 Act. Made provisions to reduce local funding fluctuation, added
remedial education to the summer youth program, allowed Governors to use certain
funds to provide technical assistance to service delivery areas, and added farmers and
self-employed to definition of dislocated worker.

Omnibus Trade and Competitiveness Act of 1988
P.L. 100-418, signed August 23, 1988, 102 Stat. 1538
Title VI, Subtitle D, the Economic Dislocation and Worker Adjustment Act (EDWAA)
revamped the dislocated worker program changing funding structure, adding rapid
response programs, ensuring funds be provided to local areas, increasing opportunities
for training dislocated workers. Also, set up the State job bank system under JTPA's
miscellaneous provisions.

Stewart B. McKinney Homeless Assistance Amendments Act of 1988
P.L. 100-628, signed November 7, 1988, 102 State. 3256
Title VII, Subtitle B created the Jobs for Employable Dependent Individuals (JEDI) In-
centive Bonus Program.

National Defense Authorization Act for Fiscal Year 1991
P.L. 101-510, signed November 5, 1990, 104 Stat. 1485
Title XLII amended EDWAA to include a defense conversion assistance (DCA) program
for workers dislocated as a result of reductions in defense spending.

Clean Air Act Amendments of 1990
P.L. 101-549, signed November 15, 1990 104 Stat. 2712
Title XI amended EDWAA to create the Clean Air Employment Transition assistance
(CAETA) Program to provide training, adjustment assistance, employment services, and
fees-related payments to eligible individuals adversely affected by compliance with the
Clean Air Act.

Nontraditional Employment for Women Act
P.L. 102-235, signed December 21, 1991, 105 Stat. 1806
Amended FTPA to add program requirements relating to the training, placing, and re-
training of women in nontraditional employment.

Job Training Reform Amendments of 1992
P.L. 102-367, signed September 1992, 106 Stat. 1021
Amended JTPA to place more emphasis on improvement of quality of service and targeting and prevention of waste, fraud and abuse. Created the Adult Training Program and Youth Training Program from former Training for Disadvantaged Program; established several new demonstration programs; Youth Fair Chance, Microenterprise Grants Program, and Disaster Relief Employment Assistance; and authorized the establishment of State Human Resource Investment Councils.

National Defense Authorization Act for Fiscal Year 1993
P.L. 102-484, signed October 23, 1992, 106 Stat. 2315
Title XLIV amended Title III (Employment and Training Assistance for Dislocated Workers) by creating the Defense Diversification Program (DDP) for certain discharged military personnel, terminated defense employees, and displaced employees of military contractors. Further amended Title III provisions for rapid response.

Supplemental Appropriations Act of 1993
P.L. 103-50, signed July 2, 1993, 107 Stat. 1547
Title XIII, Subtitle C, Sec. 1338 amended DDP with regards to eligibility; demonstration projects; and staff training, technical assistance, and coordination.

Goals 200: Educate America Act
P.L. 103-227, signed March 31, 1994, 108 Stat. 125
Amended Title II-B (Summer Youth Employment and t Training program) by adding "academic enrichment" as an authorized service; requiring youths assessed as needing basic and remedial education or preemployment and work maturity skills training be provided with such training; allowing SDAs to transfer up to 20% of their Title II-B funds to the Title II-C Youth Training program if approved by the Governor; and requiring SDAs to establish linkages with educational agencies.

School-to-Work Opportunities Act
P.L. 103-239, signed May 4, 1994, 1208 Stat. 568
Amended Title IV-B (Job Corps) to permit allowances for child care (i.e., food, clothing and health car for the child) to be paid to enrollees who otherwise could not participate in Job Corps, during the first two months of participation.

National Defense Authorization Act for Fiscal Year 1995
P.L. 103-337, signed October 5, 1994, 108 State. 2663
Title XI, Subtitle C, Sec. 1136-1137 amended DCA and DDP to allow the Secretary to fund these programs from funds reserved for Federal responsibilities under Title III and to expand eligibility to include certain workers dislocated due to reductions by the United States in the export of defense articles and services.

APPENDIX C: JTPA PROGRAMS AT A GLANCE

JTPA program	JTPA Title	Target group	Funding mechanism	FY1995 approp.
Adult Training	II-A	Age 22 and older, at least 90% economically disadvantaged, at least 65% "hard to serve"	Formula grants to State and local entities	$1,054,813,000
Summer Youth	II-B	Age 14-21, economically disadvantaged	Formula grants to State and local entities	1,056,328,000
Youth Training	II-C	Age 14-21, at least 90% economically disadvantaged, at least 65% "hard to serve," at least 50% out of school	Formula grants to State and local entities	598,682,000
EDWAA	III	Lost job or received notice, unlikely to return to current job or industry; long-term unemployed; self-employed, unemployed due to economic conditions or natural disaster	Formula grants to State and local entities	1,296,000,000
Defense Conversion	III-B, Sec. 325	Same as EDWAA program *and* laid off, terminated, or received notice due to reductions in defense spending or defense exports or as a result of base closures	Discretionary grants to States, substate grantees, and others	a
Defense Diversification	III-B, Sec. 325(a)	Certain members of the armed forces, certain civilian employees of DOD/DOE, and some defense contractor employees	Discretionary grants to States, substate grantees, and others	b
Clean Air Transition	III-B, Sec. 326	Same as EDWAA program *and* laid off, terminated, or received notice as a result of compliance with the Clean Air Act	Discretionary grants to States, substate grantees, and others	0
Native Americans	IV-A, Sec. 401	Indians, Eskimos, Aleuts, Native Hawaiians, or other Native Americans; economically disadvantaged, unemployed, or underemployed	Discretionary grants to tribal and other Native American groups	64,080,000

a$150.0 million appropriated in FY1991 is available for obligation through Sept. 30, 1997.

bAppropriations authorized for FY1993 only.

APPENDIX C: JTPA PROGRAMS AT A GLANCE -- continued

JTPA program	JTPA Title	Target group	Funding mechanism	FY1995 approp.
Migrants	IV-A, Sec. 402	Migrant and seasonal farmworkers and their dependents	Discretionary grants to public, private, and nonprofit organizations	$85,710,000
Job Corps	IV-B	Age 14-24, economically disadvantaged	Fed. admin. primarily through contracts with corporations and nonprofit organizations	1,099,460,000
Veterans	IV-C	Service disabled veterans, Vietnam veterans, and veterans recently separated from service	Discretionary grants to States	8,880,000
Youth Fair Chance	IV-H	Age 14-30; 16-19 for job guarantee program	Discretionary grants to communities	24,785,000
Microenterprise Grants	IV-I	Economically disadvantaged owners of commercial enterprise with five or fewer employees	Discretionary grants to States and Title IV-A grantees	2,250,000
Disaster Relief	IV-J	Eligible for JTPA dislocated workers programs, Native American programs, or migrant and seasonal farmworker programs or unemployed as result of a disaster	Discretionary grants to States	0
Jobs for Employable Dependent Individuals (JEDI) Incentive Bonus	V	States that provided training to absent parents of children receiving AFDC and/or blind or disabled recipients of SSI	Bonus payments to States	0

Discretionary grants are assistance awards in which Federal funds are allocated according to the determination of the administering Federal agency as to amounts and recipients. *Formula grants* are assistance awards in which Federal funds are allocated to States or their subdivisions according to a distribution formula prescribed by law or regulation.

APPENDIX D: JTPA APPROPRIATIONS, FY1984-FY1995
(dollars in millions)

Program	FY1984	FY1985	FY1986	FY1987	FY1988	FY1989
Title II-A:[a]						
Training for Disadvantaged	$1,886.2	$1,886.2	$1,783.1	$1,840.0	$1,809.5	$1,787.8
Adult Training	---	---	---	---	---	---
Title II-B:						
Summer Youth[b]	824.5	724.5	636.0	750.0	718.1	709.4
Title II-C:[a]						
Youth Training	---	---	---	---	---	---
Title III:						
Dislocated Workers						
EDWAA	223.0	222.5	95.7	200.0	287.2	283.8
Defense Conversion Asst.	---	---	---	---	---	---
Defense Diversification	---	---	---	---	---	---
Clean Air Transition Asst.	---	---	---	---	---	---
Title IV:						
Federally Administered Programs						
Job Corps	599.2	617.0	612.5	656.4	716.1	741.8
Native Americans	62.2	62.2	59.6	61.5	59.7	59.0
Migrants	65.5	65.5	57.8	59.6	65.6	68.5
Veterans	9.7	9.7	9.3	10.1	10.0	9.5
National Activities	61.7	61.1	58.5	78.5	81.5	68.6
Youth Fair Chance	---	---	---	---	---	---
Microenterprise Grants	---	---	---	---	---	---
Total: All JTPA Programs[c]	$3,732.0	$3,648.7	$3,312.5	$3,656.1	$3,747.7	$3,728.4

Footnotes at end of table.

APPENDIX D: JTPA APPROPRIATIONS, FY1984-FY1995 -- continued
(dollars in millions)

Program	FY1990	FY1991	FY1992	FY1993	FY1994	FY1995
Title II-A:[a]						
Training for Disadvantaged	$1,744.8	$1,778.5	$1,773.5	a	a	a
Adult Training	---	---	---	$1,015.0[d]	$988.0	$1,054.8
Title II-B:						
Summer Youth[b]	699.8	682.9	995.2	1,024.9	888.3	1,056.3
Title II-C:[a]						
Youth Training	---	---	---	676.7[d]	608.7[e]	598.7
Title III:						
Dislocated Workers						
EDWAA	463.6	527.0	557.0[f]	571.6[g]	1,118.0	1,296.0
Defense Conversion Asst.	---	150.0[h]	0	0	0	0
Defense Diversification	---	---	---	75.0	---	---
Clean Air Transition Asst.	---	---	50.0[i]	49.6	0	0
Title IV:						
Federally Administered Programs						
Job Corps	802.6	867.5	955.1[j]	966.1	1,040.5	1,099.5
Native Americans	58.2	59.6	63.0	61.9	64.2	64.1
Migrants	69.0	70.3	77.6	78.3	85.6	85.7
Veterans	9.3	9.1	9.1	9.0	9.0	8.9
National Activities	70.2	71.8	69.4	67.4	119.7[k]	76.3
Youth Fair Chance	---	---	---	50.0	25.0	24.8
Microenterprise Grants	---	---	---	---	1.5	2.2
Total: All JTPA Programs[c]	$3,917.5	$4,216.7	$4,549.9	$4,645.4	$4,948.4	$5,367.3

Footnotes at end of table.

APPENDIX D: JTPA APPROPRIATIONS, FY1984-FY1995--continued

[a]Prior to enactment of the Job Training Reform Amendments of 1992 (P.L. 102-367), Title II-A provided training for both adults and youth. Under the amendments, Title II-A will provide training for adults and Title III-C will provide training for youth.

[b]Appropriations for the Summer Youth Employment and Training program are generally spent at the *end* of a program year, that is, the summer of the following calendar year. In recent fiscal years, appropriations have included amounts to be spent in more than one summer. See table 1, p.10 for details of availability for FY1992-FY1995.

[c]Numbers may not add due to rounding.

[d]Reflects $30 million rescission from Title II-A and $20 million rescission from II-C made by P.L. 103-50.

[e]Reflects $50 million rescission from Title II-C made by P.L. 103-333.

[f]Includes $30 million supplemental appropriation (P.L. 102-368) for training in areas affected by Hurricanes Andrew and Iniki. Available for obligation July 1, 1992 through June 30, 1993.

[g]Includes $54.6 million supplemental appropriation (P.L. 103-75) to provide temporary jobs to address problems created by the midwestern floods of 1993. Available for obligation until Sept. 30, 1994.

[h]Funds transferred from DOD to DOL. Available for obligation through Sept. 30, 1997.

[i]Available for obligation Oct. 1, 1991 through June 30, 1993.

[j]Includes $35.6 million for Job Corps which was originally appropriated for FY1989 through FY1990.

[k]Includes $50 million for school-to-work programs funded under JTPA Title IV in FY1994. An additional $50 million was appropriated to the Department of Education for school to work programs. These activities are now authorized under the School-to-Work Opportunities Act of 1993 (P.L. 103-239).

Source: U.S. DOL budget justifications, FY1984-FY1995 and appropriations legislation.

APPENDIX E: OTHER SELECTED FEDERAL EMPLOYMENT AND TRAINING PROGRAMS

(dollars in millions)

DEPARTMENT OF AGRICULTURE

Program	Purpose	Funding mechanism	FY1995 approp.
Food Stamp Employment and Training Program (Food Stamp Act)	To assist food stamp recipients in gaining skills, training, or experience that will increase their ability to obtain regular employment	Formula grants to States, plus Federal/State cost sharing (equally) for operating costs above grant levels	$165[a]

DEPARTMENT OF EDUCATION

Program	Purpose	Funding mechanism	FY1995 approp.
Vocational Rehabilitation Program State Grants (Vocational Rehabilitation Act)	To provide comprehensive vocational rehabilitation services to help individuals with physical and mental disabilities become employable and to achieve economic self-sufficiency, independence, and inclusion and integration with society	Formula grants to States	$ 2,044
Vocational Education State Grants (Carl D. Perkins Vocational and Applied Technology Education Act)	To improve the quality of vocational education "with the full participation" of students who are members of "special populations," which include the disabled, the economical and educationally disadvantaged, and the limited-English proficient	Formula grants to States	962
Adult Education State Programs (Adult Education Act)	To enable all adults to acquire basic literacy skills, to enable those who so desire to complete a secondary education, and to make available to adults the means to become more employable, productive, and responsible citizens	Formula grants to States	252

Footnotes at end of table.

APPENDIX E: OTHER SELECTED FEDERAL EMPLOYMENT AND TRAINING PROGRAMS -- continued

(dollars in millions)

DEPARTMENT OF EDUCATION -- continued

Program	Purpose	Funding mechanism	FY1995 approp.
Federal Family Education Loans (FFEL)ᵇ	To provide federally guaranteed loans to support the cost of attendance at postsecondary institutions including colleges, universities, community colleges, technical institutes, and trade schools	Privately capitalized federally guaranteed loans	Not availableᶜ
Pell Grantsᵇ	To provide "foundation" grants to undergraduates to help pay for education after high school	Federal grants to eligible students	$2,360ᵈ

DEPARTMENT OF HEALTH AND HUMAN SERVICES

Program	Purpose	Funding mechanism	FY1995 approp.
Job Opportunities and Basic Skills (JOBS) Program (Social Security Act)	To enable recipients of Aid to Families with Dependent Children (AFDC) to obtain the education, training, and employment that will avoid long-term welfare dependence	Federal/State cost sharing (varying among the States); Federal share is limited to a legislated maximum	$ 1,300

DEPARTMENT OF LABOR

Program	Purpose	Funding mechanism	FY1995 approp.
U. S. Employment Service (Wagner Peyser Act)	To serve as a public labor exchange for individuals seeking jobs and for employers seeking workers	Formula grants to States	$ 846

Footnotes at end of table.

APPENDIX E: OTHER SELECTED EMPLOYMENT AND TRAINING PROGRAMS -- continued

(dollars in millions)

DEPARTMENT OF LABOR -- continued

Program	Purpose	Funding mechanism	FY1995 approp.
Trade Adjustment Assistance (Trade Act of 1974)	To provide cash benefits, training and related services, and job search and relocation allowances to workers who lose jobs due to competition from imported goods resulting from Federal trade policies	Entitlement program with funds allocated to States which administer as agents of DOL	$231
North American Free Trade Agreement (NAFTA) Transitional Assistance (Trade Act of 1974)	To provide cash benefits, training and related services, and job search and relocation allowances to workers who lose jobs due to competition from or a shift in production to Mexico or Canada resulting from NAFTA	Entitlement program with funds allocated to States which administer as agents of DOL	43

ªEstimated expenditure.

ᵇThe FFEL and Pell programs help finance students' postsecondary education and thus are not job training programs. However, both programs provide funding to students undertaking postsecondary occupational training at proprietary schools and community colleges. (An estimated 70% of community college students pursue occupational training.)

ᶜFederal funding for the FFEL program includes multi-year costs for loan subsidies and default reimbursements. It is not possible to allocate these costs to students attending postsecondary occupational training programs. One indication of the overall size of this investment is the loan volume (or loan amounts disbursed) for proprietary school students and vocational students in community colleges. For FY1994, total loan volume is estimated at $18.2 billion. Of this amount, a total of about $3.6 billion will be received by proprietary school students (comprising an estimated 15.4% of FFEL volume in FY1992) and vocational students at community colleges (70% of an estimated 6.1% of FFEL volume in FY1992).

ᵈFunding reported here reflects the proportion of Pell grants received by students attending proprietary schools (estimated at 21% in FY1991) and by vocational community college students (i.e., 70% of the 24% estimated as the proportion of Pell grants received by *all* community college students in FY1991).

YOUTH APPRENTICESHIPS: IMPROVING SCHOOL-TO-WORK TRANSITION FOR THE "FORGOTTEN HALF"

Richard N. Apling

SUMMARY

Recently, concerns have arisen bout the welfare of students who pursue little or no education after high school. This group is sometimes termed the "Forgotten Half" because about one-half of all high school students receive no further formal education beyond high school. Concerns for this group include their dramatically declining real wages since the mid-1970s and their particular difficulty making the transition from school to jobs in the adult labor force.

This report examines one of the most widely discussed programs to aid the "Forgotten Half": the youth apprenticeship. Beginning in the last 2 years of high school and possibly extending into postsecondary education, youth apprenticeships link learning in school with on-the-job training and work experience. Adult mentors guide students' experiences on the job. Students often rotate form job to job at the work site to obtain a broad view of related occupations and skills. Successful programs depend on close working relationships among schools, business, and labor. IN addition, success may depend on an independent party to assist in planning and implementing the apprenticeships.

Three overarching Federal policy issues with respect to creating a national youth apprenticeship system are:

- Should the Federal Government initiate a national youth apprenticeship program?

- Should a national youth apprenticeship program be integrated into current Federal programs, or should a new, separate program be authorized?

- Should the Federal effort proceed incrementally with demonstrations and research or move directly to a full-scale national program?

Integrating a youth apprenticeship program with an existing program reduces problems of overlap but might result in a low-visibility program with little or no funding. Authorizing separate youth apprenticeships could raise the visibility of the programs but lead to problems of coordination, duplication, and overlap with existing programs. An incremental approach to a national youth apprenticeship program allows testing various strategies before committing to a full-scale, fully funded program. A drawback is that tit is difficult to ensure that a full-scale program will emerge even if demonstrations ad research indicate that such an effort is warranted. Immediately authorizing a national youth apprenticeship program takes advantage of the apparent "window of opportunity" to create such a program. However, it runs the danger of wasting scarce resources by allocating funds to States, local governments, and school districts that are not ready to implement youth apprenticeships.

INTRODUCTION

Recently, concern has been growing about the large group of students who pursue little or no education after high school. This group is sometime termed the "Forgotten Half" because about one-half of all students do not pursue schooling beyond high school and because this Nation invests relatively few resources on these students. One concern is the difficulty this group faces in making the transition from school to work. Although there are a number of suggestions for easing this transition process, perhaps the most widely discussed is the youth apprenticeship.

Although a good deal has been written about youth apprenticeships, most of what we know comes from analyses of programs in other developed countries such as Germany, speculations on how foreign approaches might be changed to succeed in this country, and descriptions of a handful of small American demonstration programs. Given the paucity of detail about **American** youth apprenticeships, and discussion of their key elements and policy issues must be tentative. The discussion here is based on the current literature ad visits to three demonstration sites in Williamsport, Pennsylvania; Broome County, New York; and Pittsburgh. The Williamsport and Pittsburgh sites are part of the Pennsylvania Youth Apprenticeship Program. Broome County is the site for C Youth Apprenticeship Cornell's Project. This report contains quotes form teachers and other school officials, participating employers, and union members involved in these three programs. These quotes have been included to provide first-hand opinions of people working to invent American apprenticeships. Quotes are meant for illustrative purposes only and are not meant to convey a Congressional Research Service (CRS) position or to represent other demonstration programs, teachers, employers, or workers.

The report begins with an overview of what youth apprenticeship programs are - their key features and how they differ from current programs. Next the report reviews concerns about the "Forgotten Half" - including declining wages, difficulties in making the transition form school to work, and possible skill deficient - and how youth apprenticeships might address problems facing this group of students. The third major sections of the report discusses possible Federal roles for implementing a national youth apprenticeship program - including possible modifications to current programs and creation of a separate youth apprenticeship program. The report concludes by examining policy questions and issues.

YOUTH APPRENTICESHIPS

The youth apprenticeship is one of the most often discussed remedies to problems facing the "Forgotten Half."[1] This section review key features of youth apprenticeships, which include:

- Authentic work experience
- On-the-job training and mentoring
- Integration of education and work experience
- Certification

In addition, three groups play central roles in carrying out youth apprenticeships:

- Schools,
- Employers, and
- Labor.

Finally, although perhaps not an absolutely necessary element, outside or "catalytic" organizations may perform an important role in ensuring the success of youth apprenticeships. This section also discusses how youth apprenticeships might resemble and differ from three current Federal programs:

- Tech-Prep
- Cooperative Education
- Job Training Partnership act (JTPA)

WHAT ARE YOUTH APPRENTICESHIPS?

Youth apprenticeships link learning in school with work experience by integrating academic instruction with work-based learning and work experience taking place on the job. Perhaps the key element is the apprentice's work experience where he or she applies what is learned in school and , as a result, deepens the understanding of acquired skills and knowledge. In addition to teaching skills for a specific job and general "employability" skills (such as timeliness, effective communication, and conscientious-

---

[1] The youth apprenticeship is but one of several programs and approaches advocated to improve th etransiton from school to work. Another progam is the career academy. Career academies are "schools within schools" that foucs on one occupational cluster, e.g., healt chare, banking, or insurance careers. Career academy teachers consult with sponsoring employers in developin curriculum; the academy may contain simulted work settings; and emplouers often employ students in summer jobs. In operation for two decades, some of th ebetter known acaemies are located in Philadelphia, New York, Los Angeles, and Oaklancd. For a discussio of the Philadelphia academies, see Hayward, Becky J., Nancy E. Adelman, and Richard N. Aplling. Exemplary Secondary Vocational Education: AN Exploratory Study of Seven Programs. Discussion Papers for the National Assessment of Vocational Eduacation. Washington, Fe. 1988. For an overview of other approaches to improve shcool-to-work trnasition, see U.S. Department of Education. Office of vocational and Adult Education. Combingn School and Work: Options in High School and Two-year Colleges. Washington, Mar. 1991. Also, see Youth Apprentichships: Can They Improve the School-to_work Transition? CQ Researcher, v. 2, no. 39, Oct. 23, 1992. p. 905-928.

ness), youth apprenticeships aim to enhance academic learning and fosters positive attitudes toward work - including working as an adult in an adult workplace., Adult mentors guide students' experiences on the job, and students often rotate from job to job at the work site to obtain a broad view of related occupations and skills.[2] These programs can originate in 10th grade or earlier with career exploration to investigate occupations and clarify students' career goals. The actual apprenticeships often start during the last tow years of high school and may continue into postsecondary institutions. Program completes might proceed directly into the workforce, to postsecondary education, or even to "adult" apprenticeship programs.

Based on European models, youth apprenticeships differ in important ways from traditional American adult apprenticeships. Historically, apprenticeships in the Untied States have been essentially private-sector programs serving workers in their mid-to-late 20s who have been out of high school for several years. In addition, American apprenticeships usually focus on traditional skilled occupations such as construction trades.[3] Youth apprenticeships, by comparison, serve high-school age students and incorporate a broader range of occupations in, for example, banking and health care.

Advocates of youth apprenticeships acknowledge that European models must be adapted before they will succeed in this country. German apprenticeships, for example, appear to be too rigid and the training too narrow for the American educational system and labor markets. German students must choose early in their educational careers between apprenticeship training and university education. Moreover, students must make early decisions on a specific occupation. While change to an apprenticeship n a different occupation is possible, it means that the apprentice must start all over again at the beginning of the training, even if the two occupations are closely related.[4]

---

[2] For example, Sears sponsors an apprenticeshp prgram for appliance repari. Apprentices first spend time in the parts department (for first-hand experience in mainting inventroy ad filling orders) before they begin their repai training.

[3] For furhter information about U.S. apprentichesps, see U.S. Library of Congress. Congressional Research Serivice. Apprentichsip Training inAmerica Under the "Fitzgerald Act" (1937-1991): Policy Issues for the 102d Congress. Issue Brief No. IB91092, by William G. Whittaker, May 12, 1992 (updated regularly). Washington, 1991; and U.S. Library of Congress. Congressional Research Servicwe. Apprenticeship Training: Proposed Department of Labor Regulations. CRS Report for Congress No. 90-606E, by William G. Whittaker. Washington, 1990. 18 p.

For further discussion of the contrasts between "traditional" American apprenticeships and youth apprenticeships, see National Alliance of Business. Real Jobs for Real People. An Employer's Guide to Youth Apprenticeships. Washington, June 1991. p. 9.

[4] For a brief overiew of European apprentichsip systems, see Hamilton, Stephen F. Apprenticeshps for American Youth? TransAtlantic Perspective, no. 25, spring 1992. p. 6-9.

Another reason that the German system could not be easily trnaplanted to this country is becasue we lack and could not easily establish "the elaborate set of instituions, laws, and social norms that evolved over the course of centuries and now sustain the German eapprenticeship system." U.S. Department of Education. Office of Vocational and Adult Education. Combining School and Wrok: Options in High Schools and Two-year Colleges. Washington, Mar. 1991. p. 10.

Current attempts to design American versions of European youth apprenticeship programs are in the early stages. The U.S. Department of Labor (DOL), the Chief State School Officers, and Jobs for the Future (a nonprofit organization in Massachusetts) are sponsoring demonstration efforts.[5]

> Key elements of a youth apprenticeship program are: authentic work experience, on-the-job training and mentoring, integration of education and work experience, and skill certification.

These attempts are small and new - programs we visited enrolled between 20 and 40 students and most programs are in their first or second year of operation.

Because United States apprenticeship programs are in the pilot or demonstration phase of development, no one cannot determine with certainty whether youth apprenticeships will work well in this country'; what problems will be confronted in implementing a national program; or whether the youth apprenticeship is just another fad in American education. At the same time, both the literature on youth apprenticeships[6] and information from operating programs suggest several key elements of youth apprenticeships.

"REAL" WORK EXPERIENCE

Most high school students' jobs are low skilled and repetitive, offering little opportunity for learning or advancement. Youth apprenticeships are designed to provide quite a different work experience. Youth apprentices work along side adults in adult work settings like hospitals, banks, and manufacturing plants. While not replacing the adult worker, the apprentice performs authentic adult work. A description of the duties of a biomedical technology apprentice in the Broome County, New York, program provides some notion of the complexity and diversity of the jobs youth apprenticeship programs strive to provide:

> Youth apprentices will be trained to service the biomedical hospital equipment. Youth will observe and assist the technicians as they maintain and repair noncritical, life support and patient contact equipment, perform preventive maintenance, perform electrical safety surveys, and maintain a safe and orderly work area.

---

[5] DOL is sponsoring several school-to-work demonstration projects through: the Pennsylvania Departmetn of Commerce (Pennsylvania Youth Apprenticeship Project); the Boston Private Industry Council (Project ProTEch); the maryland Department of Economic and Employmetn Developmetn (Project MechTech, TEch-Prep Plus, and maryland's Tomorrow); Los Angeles Unified School District (Workforce LA Youth Academy); Electronic Industries Foundation (Center of Excellence in Electronics Tranining); Natioanl Alliance of Business (joint effort of Bank of America and San Francisco's Mission High School and Du-Page County/Sears School-to-work Transition Project).
The Chief State School Officers and DOL are sponsoring State-level youth apprenticeship planning in California, Maine, Minnesota, West Virginia, and Wisconsin.
Jobs for the Future is sponsoring several demonstraiton projects in Cambridge, Massachusetts, Broome County, New York, Comstrock, Michigan, Tulsa, Okalhoma, Oakland, California, Easley, South Carolina, Pasadena, California, and Portland, Oregon.
Several Stats - including Arkansas, Oregon, and Wisconsin - have legistlation authrizing youth apprenticeships.
[6] See, for example, Lerman, Robert Il, and Hillary Pouncy. Why America Should Develop a Youth Apprenticeship System. Progrss Policy Insitutue Policy Reprt, no. 5, Mar. 1990. p. 114; and Hamilton, Stephen F. Apprenticheship for Adulthood: Preparing Youth for the Future. New York, The Free Press, 1990.

This apprentice assists the biomedical technician in repair and maintenance of real machinery. He or she does not do this alone, and certain critical repairs are beyond the scope of the apprentice's activities. At the same time, the apprentice obviously performs complex and varied work under the supervision of a training adult.

STUDENT-MENTOR RELATIONSHIP

Not only is the work experience challenge, but youth apprentices do more than work - they receive most to their specific occupational training on the job. This training is done by one or more adult employees of the company hiring the apprentice. The Broome County program has identified several roes employers and their workers must play to implement an apprenticeship program:

- Designing and managing the work experience. Design ad management includes determining the skills and competencies the apprentice must acquire; mapping out sequential activities to teach these skills; coordinating job rotation to continue skill building and to provide the apprentice with a comprehensive picture of interrelated occupations; and maintaining contact with parents and the school.

- Coaching the apprentice on how to perform tasks. Coaching includes demonstrating the skills the apprentice will need to perform assigned tasks; ;monitoring and critiquing the apprentice's performance;' and modeling good performance, for example, by thinking through decisions out loud.

- Mentoring the apprentice. The mentor's role includes socializing the apprentice to the company and the adult work world; helping him or her solve problems encountered in the workplace; and advising on career decisions.

One person might fill all these roles for one apprentice - especially in a small business. Other apprentices - perhaps in larger organizations - would have several adults filling these roles. In either case, the quality of the apprentice's work experience will depend on how well the mentor and job coach can do their jobs.

INTEGRATION OF EDUCATION AND WORK

Not only is an apprentice a worker, but he or she is simultaneously a learner. For the apprentice to successfully play both roles, education and work must e integrated. That is, what is learned at school must support and reinforce both what is learned on the job and how well the apprentice performs his or her job. The integration of an apprentice's school and work experience could have the most payoff and be the most difficult aspect of youth apprenticeship programs. The pay off would come when students see the connection between what they learn at school and how well they perform on the job. Seeing this connection, students are motivated to work harder in school; their achievement improves; and they eventually become more productive workers.

Integrating education and work faces several challenges:[7]

- One key to success is **curriculum development**. Standard textbooks ad curriculum material usually do not neglect practical applications. Even if some particle examples are presented, materials would still need to be tailored to specific apprentices' work experiences. For example, math modules could be related to measurement problems apprentices face on the job. But an apprentice in a hospital lab might be measuring in milliliters and grams while an apprentice in a machine shop might be measuring in hundredths of millimeters.

- Another key is **staff development**. Many teachers might not be comfortable altering their teaching methods and material. Thus, staff development becomes essential.[8] Even more crucial is staff development for workers who will be training and "mentoring" apprentices. A master machinist or hospital laboratory technician may be first-rate employees, but this does not automatically mean that they can effectively teach a high school student those skills necessary in performing on the job.

- Early **involvement of teachers, employers, and employees** in planning and training will also be a key to success. Adalman found that most schools with successful minds between academic and vocational instruction drew heavily from academic and vocational teachers' input. Analogously, successfully linking education and work will require input from those "on the front lines" both in schools ad in the workplace. Developing and imposing curriculum and methods form the outside is less likely to be successful.[9]

- Integrating academic and work experience within youth apprenticeships **will take time to implement fully.** Experience with reforms to integrate academic and vocational education suggest that this could also take as long as a decade. This in turn had implications for duration of pilot and demonstration projects. Typically a demonstration lasts for 2 or 3 years. This almost certainly will be too short a period for a youth apprenticeship program to be successfully planned and implemented.[10]

---

[7] The cahllenges facing those trying to integrate educaion and employemtn resemble challenges involcved in integrating academic and vocational eduation. See Adelman, Nancy E. The Case for Integraiting Academci ad Vocational Education. Washington, Policy Studies Associats, 1989.

[8] One potentially useful staff deveopment activity is for teachers to visit sworksites and talk with employers and employuees about skills and knowledge various jobs requrie. Teachers probably will come away from such visits with a more concrete view of the jobs apprentices will be performing. IN addition, they may actually reciev specific problems and activities that they can use in their callsrooms. Some have suggested that particpating employers should hire teachers during the summer so they can obtain indepth understanding of hte demands of th eworkplaces yout apprentices will be entering.

[9] The National Alliance of Business poiints out that a key role that employers and employees can play is conducting specific job analyses for th epostions that apprentices will fill. A thorough analysis will provide th especifica nd general skills an dknowledge neeeded for successful job performance. A detailed analysis of these needs, in turn, can inrform teachers aobut what sould be emphasized in instruciton and perhaps even in what sequence various topics should be taught.

[10] Adelman found that successful efforts to integrating academic an dvocational instruciton had been underway for 5 to 10 years. Recall that current United States youth apprenticship demonstrations are mostly inthrie first or second year; so it is unlikely that we will know how well they have succeeded for at least another 3 years.

One approach for integrating academic education d work is the project method of instruction. Two programs we visited use a project format for part of the academic instruction. Each apprentice identifies a problem or issue related to his or her work experience. For example, a student working in a hospital laboratory could investigate problems created by the hospital's solid waste. The student would then bring to bear several academic disciplines to investigate the issue: the science involved in waste management, the local history of political decisions on where to locate land fills, the economic costs of various waste management strategies, the written skills to prepare a report on the issue, and the verbal skills to make a report to staff at the hospital.

Another approach to linking schooling and work experience is thorough feedback fro employers to teachers.. In two sites we visited, employers give teachers feedback on skills to be reinforces. Mentors at one plant we visited told academic teachers that apprentices needed help with measurement. (The precision toolmaking and machining at the plant, which manufactures engines for small aircraft, requires meticulous measurement.) Teachers added emphasis on measurement to math and science courses. AT one site, the job coach for an apprentice at a hospital asked program staff when the student would be studying anatomy. The biology course at the high school does not cover much on human anatomy; so arrangements were made for the student to take a course for credit in anatomy at the local community college.

CERTIFICATE OF ACCOMPLISHMENT

IF a national system of youth apprenticeships is ultimately to be crated, a national certification process will be necessary to make training "portable." For example, a student who successfully completes an apprenticeship in health technology in New York should receive a certificate that will be recognized by an employer in any other State. The tool making trade illustrates the need for a certification process but also the problems. One employer we interviewed noted that the tool and die trade has 25 specialties. "The tool and die trade is so broad that the company across the street may have very different skill needs than I do." He foresees a "report card" of what students have learned as very important to inform future employers what the student knows ad what he or she must be taught to assume a machinist's job at a different plant. The National Alliance of Business recommends simple checklists so that apprentices' mentors or advisors can easily indicate to the student, to teachers, and to future employers the skills that have been mastered. These check sheets can be distilled from detailed analyses of skills and knowledge each job requires.

KEY PARTICIPANTS IN YOUTH APPRENTICESHIP PROGRAMS

Clearly, schools, employers, and labor are each crucial parties for successfully implementing a youth apprenticeship. But it is also important that different groups and individuals within each of these "stakeholders" must be involved and committed for youth apprenticeships t succeed. In school districts, the superintendent and the school board must provide leadership and support (both monetary and institutional) for the program. Principals must oversee efforts within their schools to revise curriculum, plan and conduct staff development, select students, and change schedules for the apprenticeship program to succeed. Guidance counselors are important for encouraging students to consider youth apprenticeships, helping them prepare for the program, and overseeing their progress through the apprenticeship. Finally, teachers must support the program.

As one school administrator told us "Teachers have the ultimate veto power. Once they close their doors, they do what they want."[11]

From the **business perspective**, the chief executive must accept and support the program. In small businesses this may be sufficient. We interviewed several presidents of small businesses who had apparently unilaterally (or after consulting with a few other key people) opted to join the program. In larger companies with many more levels of management, a unilateral decision might not be enough. Staff of one youth apprenticeship program told us that it took them more than 2 years to convince the largest employer in the community to support apprentices. The main reason for this was that mangers at several levels - not just the chief executive - had to comprehend the program, understand their responsibilities, and lend their **active** support.[12]

Workers' support is also a key, not only because some workers will serve as coaches and mentors but also because all workers must accept the presence of high school students in their worksite. If workers are convinced that apprentices will get in the way or threaten their jobs, an atmosphere unconducive for learning can develop. If the company is a union shop, obviously union leadership must be closely involved in planning the program. In one site we visited, local unions in some companies were hostile to the concept of youth apprenticeships and program organizers could not even make appointments to talk with them. In another plant where the local president was closely consulted on implementation, the program appeared to be working smoothly.

"CATALYTIC" ORGANIZATIONS

In addition to schools, business, and labor, it may be necessary to have a fourth organization involved - one that serves as a catalyst to help plan and implement the youth apprenticeship program. In the three sites we visited, an outside organization or group appeared to be essential in starting and maintaining the program. In Broome County, it was Cornell University and Cornell's cooperative extension service. The Pennsylvania sites have regional "technology extension programs" that play this role.

A "catalytic" agency may have the expertise, resources, and detachment to accomplish important tasks that schools, business, and labor unions are not equipped or motivated to accomplish. In general, school people and business people speak different languages and see the world from very different perspectives. An outside party can help "translate" communication between the world of business and the world of education.

---

[11] One of the youth apprenticeship prgrams we visited has intitiated in-school committes to help ensure involvement from multiple levels. Composed of a district adminsitror, a school administrator, a guidance counselor, three acaemic teachers (science, math and English), a vocational educatin teacher, a aprent, and a representative form the project, these committees oversee the program at the school level, resolve shool-level problems, and serve as a sounding board for the apprentices.

[12] Employers attitudes toward and understaning of apprenticeship training will clearly influence the quality of hte work experinece. In one program we visitied, one employer said he would not allow his apprentice to perfrom producitn work. Instead the apprentice would observe workers, put away tools, and even clena up and sweep the floor. "He will get exposure to the kind of work we do, be a helper, leanr the jargon. I don't expect to get much from a 16 year old." another employer paticpating in ht esame program planned to put his apprentice to work on the producitn line but under close supervision. He and other employers int he vicintiy planned to trade apprentices during the year. Since each plant is small, rotating from site to site would expose each aprmetice to a broader range of machnery and experiences than he or she would have in one plant. This employer, who had experience training apprentices, expected them to break tools but sees his involvement as an investmetn in the community.

We saw several examples of how this "outside" agency had the time and resources to accomplish what needed to be done. The Cornell cooperative extension office was instrumental in obtaining New York State Regent's credit for apprenticeship participants. Because the State did not initially grant youth apprentices in the Broome County program Regents' credit for program participation, a student in the program might not receive the more prestigious Regents' diploma. Project staff successfully negotiate with the State so that students now receive Regents' credit for participating in the apprenticeship in their junior and senior years. The office also negotiated between and among businesses, the State's DOL, and the U.S. DOL on ambiguities in child labor laws.

In Pittsburgh, the Technology Development and Education Corporation played a number of important roles. The local project manager of the Pennsylvania Youth Apprenticeship Program recruited school districts ad employers for the project. She was responsible for publicizing the program so that parents and student knew about it. She also recruited students for the program by making initial presentations in participating schools, helping students with resumes and interviewing skills and taking students to interviews. (Employers made final selections of the apprentices they hired.) Finally, she worked with employers to help them devise training plans and helped train mentors.

How Do Youth Apprenticeships Resemble and Differ from Current Programs?

The Federal Government currently operated several program that aim to improve the education, training, and ultimate workforce experiences of populations that youth apprenticeships might serve. The design ad implementation of a national youth apprenticeship program in this country must consider how youth apprenticeships might augment as well as duplicate and overlap with these programs. This report examine three programs: Tech-Prep, Cooperative Education, and JTPA.

> A successful youth apprenticeship system I this country must consider how youth apprenticeships augment as well as duplicate and overlap current programs with similar goals, serving similar populations.

Tech-Prep

In 1990 the Congress created the Tech-Prep program as part of the reauthrization of the Carl D. Perkins Vocational and Applied Technology Education Act. Congress appropriated $104 million for Tech-Prep for FY 1993. Tech-Prep programs have the following reauthorization:

- The program coordinates a student's last 2 years of high school with 2 years at a community college or with other postsecondary educational experience ad integrates vocational and academic education.

- The high school phase concentrates on academic preparation and introductory occupational courses to ensure that students are prepared to purse more advanced training at the postsecondary level.

- In the postsecondary education phase, students pursue more advanced academic work and occupational specific courses.

- Students earn a 2-year degree in an occupational specific field.

Like Tech-Prep, youth apprenticeships may have a 2-plus-2 configuration. That is, programs enroll students in the last 2 years of high school and 2 years of postsecondary education. both Tech-Prep and youth apprenticeships aim to integrate academic and occupational courses. One major difference is that work experience is a centerpiece of apprenticeship programs while Tech-prep programs may not include work experience at all. In addition, youth apprenticeships involve business and unions as key components of the program; whereas, the main planners of tech-Prep programs are consortia of school districts and postsecondary institutions.

COOPERATIVE EDUCATION

Cooperative education (coop) is a long-standing program in both high school and post-secondary education. For FY 1992, Congress specifically appropriated $13.8 million for cooperative education under title VIII of the Higher Education Act. Like youth apprenticeship programs, coop education provides paid work experience linked to the occupational programs students are pursuing. As with an apprenticeship, the student works on the job part time (perhaps in the afternoons) and attends classes the remainder of the week.

The General Accounting Office (GAO) has identified several features of cooperative education program, which may also typify outstanding youth apprenticeship programs:

- Agreement among employers, students, and schools on specific training plans that detail general and specific skills coop students are to acquire;

- Student screening to assure that they can meet employers' requirements;

- Employers selected who can provide training in fields with potential for advancement in a career;

- Fidelity to the training plan; and

- School staff's close supervision of students at worksites.[13]

Coop programs and youth apprenticeships also differ in important respects. Coop programs are usually the culminating coursework that a vocational education student takes after 2 or 3 years of occupationally specific training. On the other hand, the first exposure to occupational specific training students in youth apprenticeships receive usually occurs on the job, and most of the occupational training takes place on the job. In addition, youth apprenticeship differ in that work experience is more closely integrated with academic instruction. Finally, high school coop programs terminate at high school graduation rather than continuing into postsecondary study as do some youth apprenticeship programs.

JOB TRAINING PARTNERSHIP ACT[14]

The JTPA is the Nation's primary employment and training program for **disadvantaged** adults and youths. In the program year ending June 30, 1991, JTPA provided training

---

[13] U.S General Accounting Office. Transition From School to Work: Linking Educationa nd Worksite Tranining. Reprot to Congressional Requresters, GAO/HRD-91-105, Aug. 1991. Washington, 1991. p.4.

[14] Ann Lordeman (CRS-Education and Public Welfare Division) wrote this section.

and related services to approximately 103,900 high school students. Of these, an estimated 6.5 percent participated in school-to-work activities.[15] In 1992, Congress amended
JTPA to create separate programs for adults and youth[16] to broaden opportunities for
collaboration between JTPA, local school system and other community resources.[17] The
JTPA is primarily administered by localities thorough subcontracts with a variety of
providers, including schools and community colleges. Each locality must have a Private
Industry Council (PIC) that provides policy guidance and oversight for the local JTPA
job training activities. A majority of PIC members must be representatives of the private
sector.[18]

The JTPA, as amended, includes three programs, components of which have similarities with youth apprenticeship programs. **The Youth Training Program**, funded at
$696.7 million for FY 1993, provides training ad related services to economically disad-
vantaged youths who meet income eligibility criteria.[19] Before local programs can provide services, they must assess participants' skills, needs, and interests and develop individual service plans to meet their needs and interests.[20] Depending on the results of
the assessments, the direct training services that could be provided and that might resemble youth apprenticeships include: programs that combine workplace training with
related instruction, preapprenticeship programs, mentoring, school-to-work transitions
services, and school to apprenticeship transition services. IN addition to direct training
services, programs also provide training-related and supportive services - such s transportation and bonuses based on attendance and performance - which may enable some
students to participate in youth apprenticeships.

The State Education Coordination and Grants Program requires each State to set
aside 8 percent of its Youth Training Program allocation for allotment to any State education agency for projects that provide school-to-work transition services and to facilitate coordination of education and training services. These school-to-work transition
services could resemble youth apprenticeships. Specifically, the Governor's coordination
and special services plan, which is submitted to the Secretary of Labor for approval,
must include with respect to school-to-work transition services: a description of the activities and services that will result in increasing the number of youth staying in or returning to school and graduating from high school; the work-based curriculum that will

---

[15] U.S. Department of Labor. Job Training Quarterly Survey. JTPA Title II-A and II Enrollmetn and Termination
During Program Year 1990 (July 1990-June 1991). Jan. 1992. Table 9. Washington, 1992; and JTPA Program
Highlights. Data From the Job Training Quarterly Survey, v. 1, no. 1. Washington, July 1992. p. 8-9.

[16] As originally enacted in 1982, JTPA provided services to economically disadvantagd adults and youth
through two prorams: the title II-A adult and youth progam and the title II-B sumemr youth emoloyemtn and
training program. Under JTPA, as amended, title II-C provides year-round services exclusively to youth; the title
II-A program provides year-round services exclusively to adutls. The 1992 amendments (P.L. 102-367) are effective July 1, 1993. U.S. Congress.

[17] U.S. Congress. Senate. Committe on Labor and Human Resorces. Job Training and Basic Skills Act of 1992.
Reprot to accomapny S. 2055. Senate Report No. 102-264, S. 2055, 102d Cong., 2d Sess. Washington, GPO, 1992.
p. 47.

[18] Other members include reprensetatives of organized labor, comminty-based organiations, educational agencies, vocational rehabilitation agencies, public assitance agencies, economic development agencies and the pulic
employemtn service.

[19] Funds are allocatd to sTates, who set aside 18 percent for activites at the State levl,a nd allocate 82 percent to
local aras. Up to 20 percent of the funds allocated to localities can be spent on administrative costs and at least
50 percnet must be spent for direct training services; the remainder can be spent on traiing related and sup-
protive servies.

[20] The assessmetn can be provded by another program sucha s a egular high school academic program.

link classroom learning to work site experience and address the practical and theoretical aspects of work; the opportunities that will be made available to participants to obtain career-path employment and postsecondary education; the integration to be achieved in the delivery of services between State ad local educational agencies and alternative service providers, such as community-based and nonprofit organization and the linkages that will be established to avoid duplication and enhance the delivery of services among other related federally funded programs.[21]

The Summer Youth Employment and Training Program, funded at $670.7 million for FY 1993 provides a variety of services including work experience and basic and remedial education to economically disadvantaged youth ages 14-21. This program could be used to complement or supplement a youth apprenticeship program, although only youth meeting income eligibility criteria can receive services.

One key feature of JTPA that is also important for successful youth apprenticeships is the private sector's major role through the PIC in planning and monitoring program activities. One important difference between JTPA and current youth apprenticeships is that JTPA has income eligibility criteria n consequently services primarily the economically disadvantaged, which would limit the use of JTPA in developing a youth apprenticeship program for all students, regardless of family income. Another difference is that JTPA has historically proved short-term training off 4 or 5 months; whereas, youth apprenticeships are longer term programs, lasting 2 or more years.

CONCERNS ABOUT THE "FORGOTTEN HALF" AND HOW YOUTH APPRENTICESHIPS MIGHT ADDRESS THESE CONCERNS

One of the central reasons the nationally youth apprenticeship system is being considered is the view that youth apprenticeships can address problems facing students who do not pursue education after high school (the so-called "Forgotten Half"). this section discusses:

> Two fundamental problems the "Forgotten Half" face are declining real wages and difficulties making the transition from school to work.

- Who makes u[p the "Forgotten Half";
- The problems this group faces; and
- How youth apprenticeships might address these problems.

WHO ARE THE "FORGOTTEN HALF?"

The "Forgotten Half" is so called because about one-half of high school students do not go on to postsecondary education and because, as the Commission on Work, Family and Citizenship has argued, there is a "sharp disparity" between American support for college-bound youth and support for the "Forgotten Half."

---

[21] The State educaiton agency submits this description whidh is developed jointly by the State educaiton agency and the Governor for inclusin int he Governor;s coordinatin and special serives plan.

- Each student enrolled in an institution of higher education can typically expect to receive a combined public and private subsidy of about $5,000 per academic year - for each of 4 years or more...

- Youth not going on to college are starved for support. Only about 5 percent of those eligible for federally supported job training receive it, then usually for only about 4 months at a level of $1,800 to $2,300..."[22]

An estimate of about one-half of the high school population may actually understate the magnitude of the problem for some groups. It is important to realize that lower percentage of minority students receive any postsecondary education. census data or 1991 show that, while 55 percent of whites ages 25 to 29 had 1 or more years of postsecondary education, only 43 percent of blacks and only 41 percent of Hispanics achieved that much schooling.[23]

In addition, many students who begin postsecondary education complete only a small proportion of their program. For example, Norton Grubb has found that many community college students dropout, and about on quarter of these dropouts attend school for less than 5 months. he concludes that "a large proportion of noncompleters spend what can be considered trivial amounts of time in community colleges.... They may have discovered quickly that they are unlikely to complete a program, or that completion will not bring them much advantage...."[24] Thus, even among those who continue education after high school, any receive only a "trivial" amount of further education.

DECLINING REAL WAGES

Perhaps the most serious concern about students who do not pursue postsecondary education is their declining real wages. Recent data show that workers in the early stages of their workforce participation (with 1 to 5 years experience) have undergone real decreases in their wags (adjusted for the effects of inflation) since the 1970s. Those with a high school education or less appear to have fared worst. Figure 1 shows that males with only a high school diploma and 5 years of experience or less earned $9.75 in 1973 compared with $6.90 in 1991 (nearly a 30-percent decrease). Male college graduates also experienced declining wages; however the gap between high graduates' and college graduates' wages has grown. In 1973, male college graduates with 105 years of experience earned on average $3.64 an hour more than males high school graduates. By 1991, they earned $5.03 more.

Patterns for women are similar: Women with only a high school education and 1 to 5 years of experience encountered a 20 percent decrease in wages between 1973 and 1991. The gap between female high school graduates and female college graduates also grew during this period: from a $3.987 per hour "premium" for a college degree to a $4.73 per hour "premium."

---

[22] The William T. Grant Commissio on work, Fmily and Citizenship. The Forgotten Half: Pathways to Success for America's Youth and Young Families. Final Report. Washington, 1989. p. 304 (emphasisi added).

[23] U.S. Department of Education. National Center for Education Statistics. The Condition of Education, 1992. NCES 92-096, by Nabeel Alsalam, et al., 1992. Washington, 1992. p. 62.

[24] Grubb, W. Norton. Dropouts, Spells of Time, and Credits in Postsecondary Education: Evidence form Longtitudinal Surveys. Economics of Eduction Review, v. 89, 1989. p. 56.

Wages of High School and College Graduates with 1-5 Years of Work Experience, 1973-1991

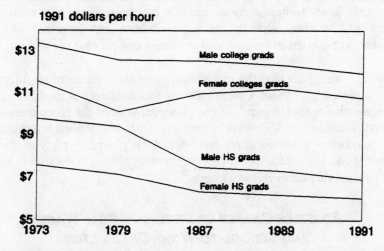

Source: Lawrence Mishel and Jared Bernstein. The State of Working America 1992-93, p. 171.

Figure 1

THE PERILOUS TRANSITION FROM SCHOOL TO WORK

Another concern is the difficulty that "non-college" bound youth face in moving from school to work. The real problem is not the transition to work - most high school students work.[25] It is the transition for jobs in he "youth labor market" to careers in the "adult labor market." The concept of a youth or secondary labor market is that high school students and those just out of high school are limited to low-skill, low-paying, low benefit, low security jobs.[26] Only as young workers approach their middle 20s do they move into the "adult" labor market.[27]

> The real problem in school-to-work transition is moving from jobs in the "youth labor market" to careers in the "adult labor market."

Hamilton and Powers make a useful distinction between the transition from school to work and the transition to career:

[25] Hamilton argues that three-quarters of all high school students are "in the labor market" - in the technical sense: one-half reprt they are working at any given time and another one-fourth say they are looking for work. he aslo argues that ahigher proportion work for some period during their high school that statistics reveal becasuse teenagers move fluidly into and out of the labor mrket. If summer jobs are included, it is reasonable to conclude that "only a small proportion of hgh school students have never been employed before graduatin." hamilton, Stephen F. Apprenticeship for Adulthood: Preparing Youth for the Future. New York, The Free press, 1990. p. 20.

[26] For a discussion of youth labor mrkets, see Osterman, Pual. Getting Started: The Youth Labor Market. Cambridge, MIT Press, 1980.

[27] Hamilton and Powers note that 44 percnet of workers 16 to 19 are employed in retail trades while 14 precnet of those older than 25 are employed in this kind of job. Hmailton, Stephen Fl, and Jnae Levine Powers. Failed Expectations: Working-Class Girls' Transiton from School to Work. Youth and Society, v. 22, no. 2, Dec. 1990. (Hereafter cited as Hamilton and Powers, Youth and Society)

Youth make the transition from school to work in several steps, beginning with part-time and vocational jobs while they are still full-time
students. For those who do not enroll in college, the next step is full-
time for near full-time employment after the termination of high school,
and then later, in their early to mid-20s, by career-entry jobs with adult
earnings, benefits, security, and possibilities for upward mobility.
Childbearing often interrupts and prolongs this process for women.[28]

Hamilton and Powers note that the transition to careers is much more difficult for those
who only complete high school. One reason for this difficulty is haphazard career planning and career choice that depend on the idiosyncrasies of the labor market at the time
of job search. Hamiton and Powers' interview with a sample of working-class high
school girls just before graduation revealed how little planning many students do. More
than 60 percent had done little or no career planning although they were about to leave
school and presumably enter the workforce.[29]

POSSIBLE CAUSES OF DECLINING REAL WAGES
AND SCHOOL-TO-WORK DIFFICULTIES

Observers debate about why real wages are falling and why the transition form school
to work is more difficult for noncollege graduates. Many factors are likely to be part of
the explanation, including the Nation's slowed rate of productivity growth, the continuing shift from manufacturing to service industries, the diminished role of unions, and
the need for firms to hod down labor costs to compete with foreign companies. Here we
examine several possible interrelated problems:

- Skill deficiencies among high school graduates;

- Lack of motivation in high school (which could obviously be related to
  low skill levels);

- Increases in skill requirements (at least in some occupations), which would
  magnify the problem of high school deficiencies; and

- The irony that high school students possibly do not pursue some high wage
  occupations even while there are shortages of workers in those occupations.

SKILL DEFICIENCIES

Evidence of knowledge and skill shortcoming in young workers comes form a variety of
sources including employer surveys, test scores, and empirical studies. While the reliability of some sources has been questioned,[30] taken as a whole the evidence indicates

---

[28] Hamilton and Powers, Youth and Society, p. 243-244.

[29] Hamilton and Powers argue that working-class girl face even more difficulties than boys. "Female's career
choices dontinue to be constrained by perceptions of what is properly women's work and by the anteicpated
subordintion of paid employemtn to motherhood." As a resutlt, the career jobs they move into often resemble
youth jobs regarding earning asn promotions possibilities. Hamilton and Powers, Youth and Society, p. 246.

[30] It has been noted, for example, that employer surveys often elicit responsed to the particular traits included
insurvey insturmetns rather than indiacte what might be employer's real needs. Many surveys only sample
employers in particualr industries or locatlities, or perhaps just in businesses of certain size. NAtriello,Gary. Do

that knowledge and skill shortcomings in young workers are likely to be widespread. Three shortcomings are often mentioned:

- **Weak Academic Skills:** Young workers frequently lack adequate basic skills in reading, computation, and writing. Employers claim they must screen many applicants to find enough who would be suitable to hires. [31] Weak academic skills also make it difficult to train employees for new assignments. Some of these weakness were revealed in a 1986 National Assessment of Educational Progress (NAEP) survey of high school graduates ages 21-25: while nearly everyone could write about a job they would like, only about 40 percent could locate information in a lengthy new article; only about 20 percent could state in writing the argument made in a lengthy newspaper column.[32]

- **Inability to Apply Skills:** Even if workers have suitable academic skills, they often cannot apply them on the job. It is not sufficient to read and comprehend a safety manual, for example: it is essential to use the manual' lessons to prevent accidents. Inability to apply knowledge makes it difficult to give employees work responsibilities that are ambiguous or might change. While little is known about how workers actually apply abstract knowledge to practical problems, the NAEP survey just mentioned reveals some weaknesses: only about half of young high school graduates could enter and calculate a checkbook balance or could follow directions to travel from one location to another using a map; only about 15 percent could plan travel using bus or flight schedules, and only 5 percent could estimate costs using grocery unit-price labels.[33]

- **Poor Work Attitudes:** Perhaps employers' most frequent complaint about young workers is their poor attitudes toward work. A Louis Harris survey "found that dedication to work and discipline in work habits were the biggest deficits that employers saw in high school graduates who wee applying for jobs."[34] A Committee for Economic Development survey of Fortune 500 companies and 6,000 smaller firms found that young workers often did not strive to work well, communicate, set priorities, work with others, or learn how to learn.[35]Poor work attitudes may be caused in part by young adults' lack of commitment to employers due to uncertainty about their careers. They may also reflect limited work experience with older adults. Whatever the explanation, poor work attitudes also make employers reluctant to invest in training young workers.

We Know Waht Employers Want in Entry-Level Workers? NCEE Brief. National Center on Education and Employemtn, Columbia University, Apr. 1989.

[31] For example, one eplyuer we interviewd sais he uses a self-developed tests to assess job applicants' skills. Although the test was desingd ot meausre eighth grade math, "70 percnet couldn't pass it, " he said. He belives that students in hgih school do not see the real-world appliactions of the subjeects they are being taught.

[32] Barton, Paul E., and Irwin S. Kirsch. Workplace Comptetnecies: The Need to Improve Literacy and Employemtn Readiness. U.S. Deprtment of Education, 1990. p. 8. NAEP is a natinally representative survey. (Hereafter cited as Barton and Kirsch, Workplace Competencies)

[33] Barton and Kirsch. Workplace Competencies. p. 9-10.

[34] Cited by Peter Cappelli in Is the "Skill Gap" Really about Attitudes? National cEtner ont eh Educational Quality of the Workfoce, University of Pennsylvania, 1991. p.5.

[35] Barton and Kirsch. Workplace Competencies, p. 17-18.

LACK OF MOTIVATION IN HIGH SCHOOL

Students' lack of effort in school may, in part, account for current skill levels. Nancy Adelman paints a vivid picture of high school students:

> They are the average students who hang on through four years of high school, apparently adding little to their academic achievement levels as a result. Whether or not their personal aspirations include further education or a job right after high school, they are kids who are going through the motions, spinning their wheels, with one (half-closed) eye on enduring until they can "get out" and a second, much more alert eye on the enticing adult world that they will shortly enter....A large part of their laziness, intransigence, or anti-intellectualism seems to stem from not seeing the point of abstract academic learning....Most...could do the work if they were motivated. For them, "Because you'll need it later" is simply not an acceptable answer to the age-old question "Why do we have to learn this?"[36]

Much of the evidence that high school students only do enough to "get by" comes form impressions and anecdotal data. For example, reporters form the Washington Post found in interviews and polls of students and teachers at a prestigious Montgomery County, Maryland, public high school that nearly 50 percent of students said they were "just sliding by" in school. The reporters' data indicated possible reasons: Two-thirds said that schoolwork is sometimes, seldom, or never meaningful and important. Nearly 50 percent believed that some, very little, or none of what they were being taught would be useful in later life.[37]

Bishop expands on this explanation: "the U.S. labor market under-rewards learning achievements in high school and that the failure to signal learning achievements to employers is at the root of the American learning deficit."[38] Although Bishop cites evidence that workers with higher skill levels are more productive, employers appear to make hiring decisions less on test cores, high school transcripts, or teacher recommendations than on years of schools, diploma obtained, and area of specialization. Apparently part of the reason for not using objective measures of skills is their unavailability to employers.

INCREASING JOB SKILL REQUIREMENTS

Analysts disagree on the extent to which job skill requirements are increasing. Some contend that the requirements of jobs are increasing.[39] To the extent this is true, it would

---

[36] Adelman, Nance E. The Case for Inteegraing Academic and vocational Educatin. Washington, Policy Studies Associates, 1989. p. I-8, I-9

[37] Leff, Lisa. Even at B-CC [Bethesda-Chevy Chse High School], the Temptation is Just to Slide By. Washington Post, Apr. 5, 1992. p. A22.

[38] Bishop, John. Incentives for Learning: Why American High School Students Compare so Poorly ot Their Counterparts Overseas. In U.S. Commission on Workforce Quality and Labor Market Efficiency. Investing in People. Background Papers, v. 1, Sept. 1989. Washington, 1989. p. 5-6.

[39] One president of a small manufacturing palnt told us tha the workplace is changeing. "The 'waist-down' skills are not as important. Even in small businesses, we are goint to CNC (computer-numerical controlled) equipmetn. These need intellignet workers to run them."

exacerbate the impact of declining student skills and widen the gap between the skills students bring to the workplace and the skills jobs require. Peter Cappelli of the University of Pennsylvania - using measures of job skill requirements in 1978 and in 1986 - finds that skills required for most manufacturing jobs (such as electricians and tool-and-die makers)have increased.[40] Increased Skill requirements may result, in part, form reorganized manufacturing processes that five workers broader responsibilities, such s ensuring product quality, which require more advanced skills in thinking, statistical control, reasoning, analyzing, and problem-solving.

Others question the extent to which companies are moving to so-called high performance workplaces and suggest that the failure to modernize the organization of work supports the demand for low-skilled workers. A recent report argues that 'the U.S. workforce lags behind in skills because U.S. companies continue to organize work in ways that depend upon low-skill jobs. Any solution to the manufacturing skills gap must treat the demand side as well as the supply side."[41] The report concludes that "the decision to underinvest in training can appear rational form the standpoint of the individual company....A company can remain extremely profitable by following the low-wage , low-skill path. But such a strategy is disastrous for the economy as a whole."[42]

An often-cited cause of increased skills requirements is the impact of technology on the workplace; however the effects of technology on skill requirements is complex. For example, advances in technology may reduce skill requirements for some jobs if new machines perform more complex tasks. Consider how supermarket scanners simplify work for both check-out clerks and managers who monitor sales and inventory.[43]

Perhaps the most that once can conclude about changing skill requirements is that it varies from industry to industry and even form company and to company. Levine concludes "that the extent of the skill transformation is uncertain and mixed: studies have fund evidence of varying degrees of upskilling and deskilling; and , they have found evidence of upskilling for some blue-collar workers (e.g., those already with high skills levels) and of deskilling for others (e.g., lesser skilled production workers)."[44]

AVOIDING HIGH SKILLED JOBS

Another concern is that high school students are no longer choosing high skilled and relatively high paying blue-collar jobs, even though employers have trouble filing vacancies. In one manufacturing plant, the director of human resources reported that his workforce of skilled machinists average 50 years of age with 18 to 45 years of experience. He is having real difficulty finding young workers with the training to qualify for

---

In Pittsburgh, on school official pointed out that "in the early 60s kids could drop out of high schoo, go to wrk for U.S. Steel, and be earning more than their high school teachers in 2 months. those jobs are no longer available, but many kids still belive they can be steel workers."

[40] Cappelli, Peter. Are Skill Requirements Rising? Evidence from Production and Clerical Jobs. Naational Center on the Educational Quality of the Workforce, Universiy of Pennsylvania, 1991.

[41] Jobs for the Future. New Training strategies for a High Performance Metalworking Industry. Report of a Conference. Cambridge, 1991. p. 5.

[42] Ibid., p. 11.

[43] For a discussion of whether techonology tends to increase or d3crease skill requiremtnsf or jobs, see Rumberger, Russell Wl, and Henry M. Levin. Schooling for ht e Modern Workpalce, In U.S. Commission on Workfoce Quality and Labor Market Effienccy. Investing in Peiole. Background papers, v. 1. p. 98-105.

[44] U.S. Library of Congress. Congressional Research Servies. The Changing Skill Requiremtns of Manufacuring Jobs. CRS Report for Congress, No. 92-642 E, by Linda Levione, Washington, 1992. p.1.

skilled jobs in his plant. In 10 years, when many in his current workforce retire, he is concerned that he will not have qualified workers to replace them.

Evidence for and explanations of this trend are anecdotal. one explanation we heard from many who we interviewed is parents' desire for their kids to go to college. They see college education as the means for their children to do better than they did. High school counselors apparently share this view and often direct even marginally prepared students to 4-year colleges.

Another problem is students' lack of understanding and knowledge about jobs and the labor market. Several people pointed to TV images driving students to certain occupations (which may look glamorous but offer few opportunities). For example, many students apparently are interested in law enforcement and emergency rescue, perhaps influence by "real life" television shows. lamenting this trend, one teacher told us, "We don't need L.A. Law, we need L.A. Machine Shop."

An additional disincentive for pursing occupational training is that students in some areas of the country must leave their "home" high school to take occupational specific courses at an area vocational technical school (AVTS). Many students do not want to do this because it requires traveling to a different site and interferes with extra-curricular activities and jobs. In addition, students attending AVTS's sometimes can be branded as not the brightest in the school, which in turn discourages students from pursuing courses at those schools.[45]

ADDRESSING PROBLEMS FACING THE "FORGOTTEN HALF"

Because American youth apprenticeship programs are in very early stages of development, it is impossible to conclude with certainty how successful they will be. At the same time, proponents of youth apprenticeships have discussed how fully implemented programs might address problems facing the "Forgotten Half," such as declining skill levels, lack of motivation in school, poor work attitudes, and inadequate knowledge about career options.

> Successful youth apprenticeship problems may raise skill levels and ease the transition to work. It is less certain these programs alone will raise wages for youth completing apprentice programs.

Principal features of a youth apprenticeship include on-the-job training and "real" work at the job site interconnected with academic, and possibly technical, education provided at the school. Ideally, the job and school experiences shod be mutually reinforcing: On the job, the apprentice realizes the importance of academic knowledge and technical skills to performing the current job and advancing to better jobs. In turn, realizing that what is learned in school might have practical applications on e job motivates the apprentice to work harder in school. As a result, the apprentice's school achievement improves. Improved knowledge and technical skills to performing the current job and advancing to better jobs. In turn, realizing that what is learned in school might have practical applications on e job motivates the apprentice to work harder in school. As a result, the apprentice's school achievement improves. Improved knowledge and skills result in improved performance on the job. Obviously, this is an idealized model of an apprenticeship program; but it illustrates the reasoning proponents use to argue that

---

[45] An employer we interfiew sees voatinal educatin as a "dumping gurnd." "I ahven't hired anyone form a vocatinal school in 10 years becasue bright kids are no longer coming form theres." Insted he hres "college dropouts" wiht no machine shop experience and trains them on site. Hew ould like to start with younger studnets and sees youth apprenticeships as another possible training gournd for machinists.

apprenticeship programs can re-engage many students in school work and , in turn, improve their achievement. Moreover, not only are academic skills improved, but the integration of schooling and work experience can improve students' ability to apply abstract knowledge in practice settings.

Another principal feature of youth apprenticeships is the coaching and mentoring the apprentice receives form one or more adult workers. The mentor not only trains the apprentice but socializes the apprentice to he world of adult work. One barrier to a smooth transition from school to career is that many high school students have little exposure to adults ad adult workplaces. I school and in social settings they are mostly influence by their peers. Even on the job (if it is typical of most "youth labor market" jobs), there is little exposure to adults and adult careers. When high school graduates move into an "adult" job, they may falter of rail when they do not realize that behavior they displayed in high school is unacceptable and can have permanent negative consequences, such as reprimand, demotion, and dismissal. An effective apprenticeship program can help the apprentice learn those lessons and behavior with fewer adverse consequences form a respected adult who is not a parent or a teacher.

Apprenticeships can also expose students to career opportunities they never considered or rejected. On-the-job experience can illustrate that a career that does not require baccalaureate degree can be rewarding and well paying. In addition, the apprenticeship experience can give students a clearer view of the path into the career they are interested in. Being on he job and working with adults who have succeeded in the career, the apprentice can get first-hand information on how best o enter and advance in that career. If no further formal education is necessary, the student can proceed directly into the workforce. If adults he or she works with entered their current jobs after receiving related training in the military, the student can weigh volunteering for the armed forces. If most successful workers have formal education beyond high school, the student will have additional motivation to pursue postsecondary education.

Arguably a well conceived youth apprenticeship program could improve academic achievement and job skills for successful completes. An effective program can also socialize young workers to the adult world of work, which should ease the transition from school to work. in addition, youth apprenticeships conceivable will open up job possibilities that many high school students do not currently consider and prepare them to enter these jobs.

Granting all this, however, does not necessarily mean that youth apprenticeships will guarantee high paying jobs. Even if youth apprentices complete their program with high academic achievement and occupational specific skills, employers must have a demand for such workers and be willing to pay them wages commensurate with their skills. Analysts disagree on whether high skills translate into high paying jobs.[46] Some, like Robert Reich, argue that a high skilled workforce will attract high paying jobs.[47] Others, like Lawrence Mishel, worry that many employers may have already made decisions in favor of low skills and low wages and are willing to pay these low wages to American workers or to workers in Mexico, Southeast Asia, or even countries of the former Soviet Union.[48]

---

[46] A related issue is the degree to which job skill requriemetns ar eincrasing. See apge 21 for a discussion of various views on this issues.

[47] See Reich, Robert B. The Work of Nations. New York, Alfred A. Knopf, 1991.

[48] For a discussion fo te shift to low-paying indutries, see Mishel, Lawrence and Jred Bernstein. The State of Working America, 1992-93. Wshington, economic Policy Insitutue, 1992. p. 173-180.

POSSIBLE FEDERAL ROLES

One key question with respect to a possible Federal role in creating a youth apprenticeship program is: **Should the Federal Government have any role?** Youth apprenticeship programs could develop and survive that the State and local levels without Federal encouragement or involvement. After all, State and local programs have arisen with little or no Federal support. Business concern about filling technical positions could spur the development of apprenticeships. Some business leaders already anticipate shortages in skilled occupations such as health technicians, machinists, tool and die makers, and auto body designers. They worry that traditional courses such as community colleges and the military will not produce sufficient satisfactory candidates for these jobs. Youth apprenticeships in technical areas may survive, even expand, as long as business sees a clear need for graduates of these programs.[49]

> Three fundamental questions regarding the Federal role are:
> Should the Federal Government have a role in creating a youth apprenticeship system?
> If Federal Government has a role, should a national system be created by amending current programs or creating a separate youth apprenticeship program?
> Should the Federal Government proceed incrementally with further demonstrations and research or authorize a full-scale program immediately?

If the Federal Government has some role to play in creating a national youth apprenticeship system, two overarching questions for Federal policy are:[50]

- Should a national youth apprenticeship program be integrated into existing program, or a new, separate program authorized?

- Should the Federal effort continue and expand demonstration programs, or should a full-scale effort be authorized immediately?

MODIFYING CURRENT PROGRAMS

As discussed earlier, several programs have similarities with youth apprenticeships. A possible Federal strategy for implementing a youth apprenticeship program would be to amend one or more of these programs to include a youth apprenticeship component. Three potential programs are Tech-Prep, Chapter 1, and JTPA.[51]

---

[49] A national move toward hgih-skill , high wage work places could greatly increase the demand for apprenticeship programs; however it is not clear how quickly U.S. business is curently moving in this direction.

[50] Several bills were introduced during te 102d Congress with youth apprenticeship components. None of these proposals became law. For a discusion of these proposals see U.S. Library of Congress. Congressional Research Service. Analysis of Various "Workforce Radiness" Bills Under Consideraton by the 102d Congress. CRES General Distributin Memorandum by Richard N. Apling, July 10, 1992. Washington, 1992.

[51] Cooperative Educatin is another progam that could be modified to accommodate yout aprpenticeshps; however, the ralteively small size and limtied Federal involvement sugges that coopertive educaitn migh nt be the best vehicle for ounting a natianl youth apprenticeshp prgram. Current studnet particpatin in cocop programs is relatively small. GAO reports that 4 percnet of all ghigh chool studnets ad 3 percnet of community colelge studnets particpated in coop programs in shool year 198901990. GAO Transition From School to Work, p. 16 and 19. Federa funding for cooperative educaitn is limited. Perkins Act basic State grant funds presumablyu can be used for cooperative education at either the seodnary or postsecondary level, although the lsaw does not speifically autnroize this use of funds, nor do we know how much of Perkins funding goes for cooperative education.

TECH-PREP

As previously noted, the Tech-Prep program under the Perkins Act aims to improve high school technical instruction and link high school and postsecondary learning. Current law also encourages some links between education and work. For example, Tech-Prep consortia may combine high school components with either adult apprenticeship programs or postsecondary institutions, such as community colleges. (The latter is the more likely program configuration.) In addition, "special consideration" is to be given to Tech-Prep programs that are developed in consultation with business and labor and provide "effective employment placement activities" after graduation.

Tech-Prep could be modified to strengthen links to employers and the workplace. The legislation could be modified to require that program planning be done in conjunction with local business and union leaders. The legislation could mandate that Tech-Prep programs incorporate work experiences through youth apprenticeships. The Maryland Tech-Prep Plus program is an example of combining Tech-Prep and youth apprenticeship. Tech-Prep Plus adds full-time summer work experience related to each student's specific training, and strengthens school-work connections by teacher visits to worksites and employers visits to schools.[52]

CHAPTER 1

Another program that could be modified is chapter 1 of title I of the Elementary and Secondary Education Act.[53] Funded at $6.7 billion for FY 1993, the chapter 1 program aims to improve both "basic and more advanced skills" of "educationally deprived" children. Throughout the history of the program most funds have been concentrated on basic reading and mathematics skills in elementary grades; relatively few resources have gone to high schools. One reason for this is the assumption that earlier intervention is more effective. Another reason is that there are relatively few remedial materials for high school students.

A possible modification to chapter 1 would be to expand the program in senior high schools to connect basic and more advanced academic instruction with students' work experiences. Various changes in chapter 1 could ensure increased participation by high school students and tie chapter 1 serves to occupational education and student work experience:

- Chapter 1 could be modified to make serving high school students easier.
- Chapter 1 programs could be required to serve more high school students[54]

---

funding under title VIII of the Higher Educaiton Act of 1965, as amended, for cooperative educationa is less than $14 million for FY 1993.

[52] See U.S. Departmetn of Labor. Lessons Learned From School-to_work Demonstraion Projects. [no date] p. 3-4.

[53] For further discussin of possible modificatins to chapter 1 in this regred see U.S. Library of Congress. Congressional Research Servies. Selected Reform Options for Federal educatin Policies a dthe Elementary an Secondary Educaitna Act. CRS General Distribution Memorandum by the Educatin and Public Welfare Division, Edicaiton Section. Oct. 26 1992. p. 28-31.

[54] Chapter 1 par C authrozes a separate prgram for hgih schools, which permits use of funds for "innovative", prgrams for a variety of activities including pre-employmetn and shcool-to-work transiton, but has never been funded.

- High school chapter 1 programs could integrate academic redemption and advanced academic skills with occupational courses and work experience.
- Chapter 1 high schools could also be coordinated with Tech-Prep programs.[55]
- Chapter 1 programs in high schools could be coordinated with work experiences.[56]

JOB TRAINING PARTNERSHIP ACT[57]

The Job Training Partnership Act might not need extensive modification to provide support for youth apprenticeship programs. Even though not all students in youth apprenticeship programs would qualify for JTPA, youth apprenticeships could be conducted under the three previously discussed JTPA programs: the Youth Training Program, State Education Coordination and the Summer youth Employment and Training Program. Indeed, one youth apprenticeship program we visited had used JTPA summer youth resources to fund apprentice positions during the summer for qualified youth.

The National Alliance of Business reports:

> There are no restrictions preventing JTPA-eligible high school students from participating I youth apprenticeships and , in fact, the U.S. Department of Labor-funded Maryland's Tomorrow Youth apprenticeship program is geared specifically to JTPA-eligible students. Other operators [of youth apprenticeship programs] report some difficulties in mixing JTPA-students with other students in a single program because JTPA funds must be carefully monitored to ensure that they are not spent on services to noneligible students.[58]

Perhaps the most promising connection between JTPA and youth apprenticeships is the new authority for schoolwide projects under the Youth Training Programs. Youth in the Youth Training Program do not have to meet individual eligibility requirements if they attend a public school that meets the following criteria: located n an area with a poverty rate of 30 percent of more, served by a local educational agency eligible for assistance under chapter 1 of the Elementary and Secondary Education act, with 70 percent of the students facing at least one specified "barrier to employment," (including , for example, those with basic skill deficiencies, school dropouts, and pregnant or parenting youth) and conducting a program under a cooperative agreement between the SDA and the appropriate local educational agency. In other words, localities could develop schoolwide projects for providing youth apprenticeships in high poverty neighborhoods.

---

[55] Texas is alrady coordinating theh JTPA with tech-prep ptrams. "JTPA can complement tech-prep programs by providing rememdiatein to interested applicants and support servies to those int raining and by placing graduates into jobs." Employemtn and training Reporter, July 29, 1992. p. 893. Hgih shcool level chapter 1 could play a similar role, especially regarding remeidal educatina for those interested in tech-prep programs.

[56] Most high school studnets work for pay in some capacity. See, for example, Hamilton and Powers, youth and Society, p. 245.

[57] Ann Lordeman (CRS-Education and Public Welfare Division) contributeed to this section.

[58] National Alliance of Business. Real Jobs for Real People. An Employer's Guide to Youth Apprenticeshps. Washington, Juen 1992. p. 17. (Hereafter cited as National Alliance of Business, Real Jobs for Real People)

One modification that could be made to JTPA would be to direct the Secretary of Labor to sue some of the $15 million reserved annually for capacity building, information dissemination, and replication activities to promote youth apprenticeships. A second modification would be to specifically make youth apprenticeships an allowable direct training service. A third modification would be to relax the income eligibility requirements for students participating in youth apprenticeships. This modification would enable localities to develop apprenticeships that could serve all youth, but this would be a major change away from targeting JTPA serves to the very disadvantaged.

ISSUES IN MODIFYING CURRENT PROGRAMS

A potential strength of integrating youth apprenticeships into one or more existing programs is reducing the perennial problem of coordinating job training and education programs that provide similar serves to similar populations. Even though programs overlap and coordination and cooperation apparently make eminently good sense, issues of "turf" at the Federal, State , and local levels often prevent cooperation and lead to duplicative services.[59] In addition, programs that appear to have similar purposes must compete for funding. A separate youth apprenticeship program might be authorized but not funded or funded at a minimal level - because it would be in competition for scarce resources with programs such as Tech-Prep and JTPA. Of course incorporating youth apprenticeships into one or more existing programs still does not guarantee funding.

A possible problem with modifying existing programs is that staff of these programs might see the youth apprenticeship component as an unwelcomed appendage. They might resist adding new features to a program they see as functioning well. In addition, as previously noted, adding youth apprenticeships to existing programs does not ensure funding. Moreover, authorizing youth apprenticeships through some programs such as JTPA and chapter 1 would provide access only to those who are eligible for these program, e.g., those demonstrating that they are economically disadvantaged. finally, some programs, such as Tech-Prep and JTPA, recently have been authorized or significantly amended, and some might argue that it is too soon to make major revisions to these programs.

CREATING A NEW PROGRAM

In addition to, or instead of, modifying current programs, Congress might consider authorizing a separate, new youth apprenticeship program. A major question is whether we know enough about implementing youth apprenticeships to mount a nationwide Federal program. If, as some argue, we do not, then Congress might consider a more incremental approach involving demonstration programs and research and development before authorizing a full-scale program. If, as others argue, studies and demonstration programs rarely lead to substantial and permanent changes, Congress could authorize a national competitive grant or formula grant program for youth apprenticeships.

---

[59] For a discussion of one solution to problems of coordinattion and duplication (the creation of the State Human Resource Investmetn Councils as aprt of th eJTPA Amendments of 1992), see U.S. Library of Congress. Congressional Research Service. Job Traning Partnership Act: Legistlation and Budget Issues. CRS Issue Brief No. IB91117, by Ann Lordeman and Karen Spar, Sept. 10, 1991 (update regualry). Washington, 1991.

INCREMENTAL STRATEGIES

An incremental approach to implementing a national youth apprenticeship program could include some or all of the following components:

- A national study of existing American youth apprenticeship programs[60] to identify components of success, problems to avoid, and whether and how to mount larger-scale efforts;

- Identification of successful models of youth apprenticeships (perhaps building on a national study) by the DOL, the U.S. Department of Education (ED), or some other Federal Agency, dissemination of these models to States and school districts, and provision of technical assistance to those interested in starting apprenticeship programs;

- A national demonstration, which would fund applicants to implement, modify, and evaluate models identified by a national study;

- Planning or start-up grants and technical assistance to State and local governments to encourage youth apprenticeships based on the demonstration models; and

- Federally sponsored research and development on topic such as curriculum development, occupational standards, and mentor training.

A NATIONAL YOUTH APPRENTICESHIP SYSTEM

An alternative to an incremental, evolutionary Federal role is authorizing a national youth apprenticeship program. This could be done immediately or after a national study identified lessons that could inform the Federal initiation and oversight of such grants. A national youth apprenticeship program might include the following features:

- A national program would most likely involve an intergovernmental partnership of the Federal Government, States, and local entities.

- Federal legislation and administration might set an overall framework for the program and permit substantial State and local discretion to implement the program to meet diverse economic, demographic, and educational conditions.

- A federal framework might include: State and local assurances against abuse of children and workers; guarantees of equal participation for "special groups" such as women and the economically disadvantaged; broad outlines of program configurations (for example, that youth apprenticeship programs would link the last 2 years of high school with 2 years of postsecondary training); mechanisms for aiding business-labor-education collaboration (such as authorizing outside catalytic agencies).

- A national grant program could be developed to link youth apprenticeships to other social investments, such as infrastructure restoration. For example, contrac-

---

[60] Several States and local partnerships have begun embryoinic youth apprenticeship programs. Most appear to be new and/or very small. See, for example, State of Arkansas Request for Proposal; and Hamilton, Stephen F., Mary Agnes Hamilton, and Benjamin J. Wood. Creating Apprenticeshi Oppoortunites for Youth. A Progress Report from the Youth Apprenticeship Demonstration Project in Broome County, New York, Sept. 1991.

tors receiving funds for Federal highway construction and environmental cleanup could be required to participate in local youth apprenticeship programs and employ youth apprentices as some percentage of their workforce.

- Even if a national grants program were authorized, the Federal role most likely would include other activities that would also be sponsored under a more incremental approach such as research and development, dissemination, and technical assistance.

A COMPROMISE BETWEEN THE INCREMENTAL AND FULL-SCALE APPROACHES

A possible compromise between an incremental approach and immediate full-scale implementation would be to begin with preliminary activities and paths in a national program during an initial authorization period. The program could be initially authorized for 5 years. Consortia of schools and businesses could be established. For the first year, grants would be used for planning. Specific apprenticeship occupations would be identified; detailed job analyses of these occupations would be conducted; curriculum based on the job analyses would be written; and teachers and employers would be selected and trained. The remaining 4 years, would be for implementation. States, regions, or local areas that already have apprenticeship programs could begin expansion during the first year. During the 5-year period, national studies would be conducted of existing programs. Information from these studies could inform technical assistance that the Federal Government would provide during the planning and implantation process. In addition, the national studies would inform the reauthorization process at the end of the intial 5-year authorization.

ISSUES IN CREATING A NEW FEDERAL PROGRAM

If a more incremental approach is chose, a central issue is how to ensure that a national program is initiated if evidence form demonstrations and other preliminary activities indicates that a national program is warranted. If a national program is authorized immediately, it is important to ensure that funds are not forced on States ad local participants before they are ready to spend the funds effectively.

Whenever a national youth apprenticeship program is initiated - incrementally, after a phase-in period, or immediately - several issues must be addressed:

- **Which Federal agency administers the program.** Various proposal locate a national youth apprenticeship program in different Federal agencies. One approach is to locate the program under the Bureau of Apprenticeship and Training and because DOL is sponsoring several youth apprenticeship demonstration. Other proposals would have the ED administer youth apprenticeships, in part based on the argument that these are more education programs than training programs. A third proposal would create a new independent agency (like the National Science Foundation), based on the view that no existing Federal entity is well equipped to coordinate a youth apprenticeship program. A final alternative is to make one agency responsible for administering the program and require "agreements of understanding" with other relative agencies to ensure their involvement and cooperation. The character of national youth apprenticeships is likely to be influenced by which agency oversees them. For example, a DOL-run program is likely to emphasize training and perhaps be better coordinated with DOL programs such as JTPA. An Ed effort is more likely to resemble an education program and be better coordinated with Tech-Prep and other vocational education programs.

- **Whether to authorize competitive grants or a national formula grant.** Under a competitive grants program, a limited number of States of local programs would be funded based on which submitted the best proposals. Under a formula grant, all States, even all counties or all school districts, would receive funding based on some distributional mechanism. One advantage to the competitive grant approach is that it is more likely to fund programs that are well thought out. The corresponding disadvantage to a formula grant is that it might thrust money on many who are unprepared to spend it. One advantage of a formula program is that it can be structured to focus resources based on policy considerations - for example, by targeting funding to schools with high concentrations of economically disadvantaged students. A corresponding disadvantage of a competitive grants strategy is possible unintentional targeting of resources to larger or wealthier governmental entities that can afford staff to write high-quality proposals. A possible compromise is to tie the final decision to the level of funding appropriated for the program once it is authorized. The tech-Prep programs under the Perkins act has a "trigger" of $50 million. At or below that level of appropriations, Tech-Prep is a competitive grants program run by the Secretary of Education; above that amount the Act stipulates a formula grant program for Tech-Prep.

- **Whom to fund.** There are several possibilities. For example, States could be funded directly, and the decision left to the States about substate allocations. States could be funded and directed on how to allocate funds (e.g., by formula) to consortia of schools and businesses. Alternatively funds could flow to States and the to "third party" entities. Those eligible might include, for example, universities, regional economic development agencies, and extension agencies. These grant recipients would serve as catalysts to assemble school and business participants and facilitate the planning and implementation of local and regional programs.

- **Which State agency to fund.** If funds flow to States, the question remains which State agency or agencies receive funds and oversee the youth apprenticeship program. Just as the national character of the program will be influenced by which Federal agency oversees it, the State and local character of youth apprenticeships will hinge on who is in charge at those levels. Youth apprenticeship programs are likely to resemble other education programs if funds flow through the State Education Agencies. Programs might have more of a job training emphasis if departments of labor are involved. Programs could have much more of an economic development purpose if funds go to State commerce departments. One approach is to fund programs through governors and allow them to decide which agency or agencies would administer the program.

- **Standards and certification.** As discussed previously, certifying successful completion of a youth apprenticeship is an important feature of a national youth apprenticeship system. Among other thins, certification tells employers what academic and occupational skills and knowledge the youth apprenticeship has acquired. Developing certification processes for a wide range of occupations that could be represented in a national youth apprenticeship program will be incredibly complex. Although one could argue that this should be a private sector endeavor (as it essentially is for adult apprentice programs), there are a number of roles the Federal Government could play. For example, ED and DOL have recently awarded $4.7 million in grants to 13 consortia of educational groups and trade associations to develop job-specific standards. These grants could forma component of a national certification system. Another component of such a system could be built on DOL's Secretary's Commission on Achieving Necessary Skills (SCANS), which has developed a set of general workforce skills.[61] Beyond the development of specific and generic standards, the Federal Government may have some role in developing the "infrastructure" to support a certification system. This might include: revising curriculum, textbooks, materials, ad tests to reflect these standards; training teachers to incorporate an devaluate standards in their classrooms; and persuading and educating employers to use certificates as par to their hiring processes.

- **Coordination with other programs.** As noted previously, creating a separate youth apprenticeship program raises the necessity of helping to ensure that the program is coordinated with existing job training and education programs. This has been a perennial problem. As previously discusses, the most recent attempt to deal with coordination problems is the creation of the State Human Resource Council. At the very least, authorization of a new apprenticeship program could require that it be incorporated into this council.

POLICY QUESTIONS AND ISSUES

Regardless of what role the Federal Government plays in youth apprenticeships, a series of questions and issues are likely to arise. Some issues and questions will be of most importance to particular groups. For example, school personnel are likely to be concerned about how a youth apprenticeship program might compete with (even threaten) current programs. Employers are likely to be concerned with the benefits to them of youth apprenticeship programs. Workers may be concerned about whether youth apprentices will provide a cheap source of labor that will displace current workers. In addition, there are issues and questions all parties will confront: For example, how much will the program cost? This section discusses first issues that specific groups might raise and then broader issues that arise concerning youth apprenticeship programs.

ISSUES FOR SCHOOLS AND TEACHERS

THREATS TO CURRENT PRACTICES

Youth apprenticeship programs require changes in educational practices. Academic subjects must be integrated with work experience - meaning that English, math, science, and social studies teachers must rethink and revise what and how they teach. Substantially more occupationally specific training takes place on the job, which raises questions about the role for traditional vocational education teachers. Do they support on-the-job training; concentrate on perhaps lower skill occupations (such as cosmetology) that are

---

[61] See U.S Department of Labor. Secretary's Commission on Achieving Necessary Skills. Learning a Living: A Blueprint for High Performance. A SCANS Report for America 2000. Washingtton, Apr. 1992. p. xiv.

not included in youth apprenticeship programs; or find their programs phased out altogether?

The uncertainty and change required to implement a youth apprenticeship program can produce resistance from teachers. As noted earlier, teachers have ultimate veto power if they choose not fully participate. Teachers' resistance probably can be reduced if they are meaningfully involved early in planning and implementation. In one site we visited, initial resistance appeared to result because teachers saw the program being pushed by people outside the schools, such as business leaders and other advocates of economic development. Teachers resented the implication that the educational system had failed and that "outsiders" could tell them how to fix it. Once this probably was recognized and teachers and principals were brought into the decision making process, resistance in the schools subsided to some degree.

Youth apprenticeships may require the roles of guidance counselors to change, and this can lead to resistance from that group. One teacher we interviewed pointed out that counseling is fragmented. Vocational teachers do some career counseling but only for students in their program. School guidance counselors often concentrate on scheduling and crisis management. They do little career counseling, in par, because "they know little bout the world of work." One possible strategy would be to provide opportunities for guidance counselors to regularly talk with employers and visit work sites. These discussions ad visits could help educate counselors on the opportunities open to students participating in youth apprenticeship programs. Counselors then might be motivated to begin recruiting students in earlier grades and help them select courses to prepare themselves for youth apprenticeships.

In some communities, youth apprenticeships may be competing for students with traditional school programs. In one site we visited, some principals have resisted youth apprenticeships because they see the program taking away students. Faced with declining enrollment, principals fight for 'warm bodies" to avoid losing teaching positions and other personnel. Because of principals' resistance, the program recruiter was allowed to visit less than 10 percent of the 10th grade class - those who would enter the program as juniors. She was not permitted to contact any students at one high school, which is a "magnet" school and part of the desegregation plan. School officials feared that the youth apprenticeship program would draw off students from this school and "unbalance" its enrollment.[62]

WHERE SHOULD APPRENTICES' ACADEMIC INSTRUCTION BE PROVIDED?

Another issue facing teachers and other educators is where academic instruction for youth apprentices should take place - in the students' "home" schools or in some separate facility. We found some disagreement among the programs we visited. In one program, a team teaches apprentices at a local community college. The designer of the program intentionally moved academic instruction off-site to facilitate reform. "We have to get away from 30 minute blocks of instruction," he said.

Other programs provide academic instruction in students' "home" schools. Program administrators at one site believe strongly that students should continue to pursue their

---

[62] Another possible hinderance to studnet recureitment is students' reluctance to travel to distant worksites. Becasue the program in one site we visited concetnrated on apprenteiceships in one occupatinal area and because most particpating emploiyers are outside the city, students ave to travel considerable distances without much public transportatin) to go to work. One teacher we interviewd said this would have been less of a problem if other occupations - such as health care - ahd been included.

academic instruction at their home schools. "If you separate apprentices from other students, you make the same mistake they mad in putting most vocational education in [intermediate educational units]." This has several possible disadvantages. It makes apprentices feel less a part of their high school and its extracurricular activities. In addition, transportation to and from an off-site location adds to the cost of the program. Finally, a separate program can stigmatize participants as somehow inferior to those that remain full time at the "home" school.

EMPLOYER'S CONCERNS

Obviously, youth apprenticeship programs will not succeed without employers' enthusiastic participation. At the same time, employer involvement raises several issues, both form the employers' perspective and from broader public policy perspectives. In the employers' view, are questions of costs and benefits. Employers clearly will face a variety of costs to support a youth apprenticeship program. (We discuss cost estimation more broadly below.) Employers want to know what benefits will accrue from their participation in the program. Some of the employers we interviewed see few immediate benefits to their companies or the bottom line. They are participating from a sense of civic responsibility. Others are concerned about shortages of skilled workers ad see youth apprenticeships as a long term investment to secure the future. Still others employers are willing to invest in training youth apprentices but worry that their investment may benefit their competitors: A competing company can refuse to participate in the program and simply hire the apprentices but worry that their investment may benefit their competitors: A competing company can refuse to participate in the program and simply hire the apprentices once they have completed training another company provides.

From a broader public policy perspective, the issue arises as to whether to provide incentives to employers to participate. Incentives could take the form of tax credits for employers hiring ad training youth apprentices. One argument for such incentives is that they are necessary to attract sufficient numbers of employers for a viable youth apprentice system. It is questionable whether there are enough employers available who would participate simply form a sense of civic duty or altruism. Moreover, concern with short-term returns may make employers reluctant to invest for longer term results, even if they realize they face future shortages of skilled workers.

On the other hand, incentives such as tax credits raise the program's cost to government. Moreover, they mean more paperwork for some employers, which can be a particular burden on owners of small businesses without the resources to track paperwork. One employer we interviewed was opposed for tax incentives for this reason. In addition, incentives may attract some employers for the wrong reasons; e.g., mainly to reduce tax liabilities and only secondarily to train apprentices.

ORGANIZED LABOR'S CONCERNS

REPLACEMENT BY YOUNGER, LOWER-WAGE WORKERS

Union leaders and members have expressed concern that business will use youth apprenticeship programs as a source of lower-paid, nonunion workers.[63] For example, a preliminary study in Wisconsin of youth apprenticeships reported that "many parents who belong to labor unions said they feared youth apprenticeship programs may jeopardize their own jobs, giving teenagers jobs that might otherwise go to dues-paying adult workers."[64]

Federal legislation could require assurances that youth apprentices not replace current workers or those laid off who are subject to recall.[65] But the actual implementation and safeguarding of these assurances will be necessarily be local matters, possibly requiring detailed negotiation between a particular company and its local union. Details of such agreements are likely to differ widely. (The "catalytic" agent discussed above could be instrumental in facilitating those negotiations.)

In one plant we visited, labor and management arrived at a series of informal agreements to make sure that apprentices would not be seen as "scabs". If a labor dispute ever arose, the apprentices would not be allowed to cross a picket line. In addition, the union insisted that apprentices be supervised at all times and at no time should there be any question that the apprentice was going the assigned job of a full time worker. Although youth apprentices are permitted to make parts and run machinery, they do not work in the "production Mode". For example, youth apprentices might produce 2 parts per hour while an adult worker would produce 20 per hour. One reason for the much lower rate is that the monitor is expected to stop the youth apprentice for instruction, to quiz him or her on what is being done, etc. The apprentice is permitted to run production machinery, but if the supervising worker needs to leave the work area for any reason, the machine is shut down so that the apprentice cannot produce parts on his own.

THE WORD "APPRENTICESHIP"

An additional issue form the union perspective is the term apprenticeship. To some, apprenticeship refers to traditional adult "registered apprentice" programs that traditionally have developed as established entry points into particular crafts. Unions often play a key role in these apprenticeship programs. Something called a "youth apprenticeship" can be perceived as an attempt to interfere or supplant the traditional apprenticeships in this country.[66]f

An obvious solution would be to use a different term - such as "pre-apprenticeship" - to label the program. As one union president told us, "If you changed the name from apprenticeship to something else, most of labor's problems would disappear." On the other hand, this might cause confusion. So much has been written and discussed under the rubric of youth apprenticeships that some would wonder how a pre-apprenticeship

---

[63] Arguably the concerns about youth apprenticeships that organized labor expresses may be of greater concern for workers who do not have union representation, who are the majority of the workforce.

[64] The same workers said they would like to see their own children enrolled in an apprenticeshp program. Chiefs Embrace Plan to Focus on Work-Related Education. Education Daily, Nov. 13, 1991. p. 4.

[65] For examples of assurances, see S. 2745 introduces during te 102d Congress.

[66] For further discussion, see Youth Apprenticeships: Can They Improve the School-to-Work Transition?, p. 909.

implies that the student is preparing for a full fledge apprenticeship, which is only one of the possible result of such a program.

GENERAL ISSUES

HOW MUCH DOES AN APPRENTICESHIP PROGRAM COST?

Creating a youth apprenticeship program might not be that expensive. One program coordinator told us: "We have plenty of money; the task is to reallocate it." This may be overstating the case. There almost certainly will be new costs associated with a youth apprenticeship program. Several parties must bear costs:

- Sponsoring **business** must pay the stipend of salary of the apprentices. If this is minimum wage of $4.25 per hour for 15 hours per week for a 9-month school year, the business would pay about $2,500 for each apprentice.[67] Additional (probably mostly noncash costs) would accrue for management time, worker time, space and equipment use, etc.[68]

- **Students or parents** might be expected to pay transportation costs to and from the work site. If not, this cost probably would be paid by the school system, perhaps with transportation vouchers.

- **School districts** would face costs associated with program planning and administration. Teachers participating in the program might need release time for various activities such as training a curriculum development. (For example, one superintendent we interviewed advocates release time for teachers to visit the job sites where apprentices work to learn more about the "real world" and what academic skills students apply on the job.) Teachers might also receive stipends if the apprenticeship program added to their teaching or advising load.[69]

> General concerns and issues about youth apprenticeships include:
>
> How much would a youth apprenticeship cost?
>
> How much should a youth apprentice be paid?
>
> How can abuse of youth apprentices be prevented?
>
> How should national standards be set for youth apprenticeship programs?
>
> How can equal access be provided for "special" populations such as minorities and women?

---

[67] One employer we interviewd estimated costs of $20,000 for six apprentices.

[68] The National Alliance of Business reprots that "aside from theh limited costs associted with training mentors/advisors, the costs in a well-planned apprenticeshp are not greater than those associated with the supervisio of other new employees. In fact, a number of empoloyers have noteiced that the productivity and morale fo experienced workers who act as advisors or mentors actually rise." National Alliance of Business, Real Jobs for Real People, p. 18.

[69] Hannah Roditi points out that costs to schools will depend on program design. One desing feature is student-teacher ratio. The lwoer the ratio, the higher the cost of the program. Additional duties for teachers also can add to costs. If teachers are required to spend extra time developing curriculum, counseling students, or visiting worksites, union contracts may requrie additional compensation. On the other hand, costs (to the school district, at least) could be reduced to the extent that more training is done at the worksite and provided by the employer. Roditi, Hanna Finan. How Much Does a Youth Apprenticeship Porrram Cost, and Who Will Pay for It? Jobs for the Future. Somerville, Massachusetts, Agu. 1991. p. 7.

- If a **coordinating agency** is involved, its funding might come from participating school districts and business, from the State or Federal Governments, and even form private sources.

Initial **costs per student** of a program might be high. For example, we were old in one site we visited that the program was costing more than $18,000 per student (in contrast with about $4,000 per-student for academic courses an d$6,000 for vocational education courses). However, these high per student costs appeared to be due mostly to the small number of students enrolled and the resulting low pupil-teacher ration. Staff believed that a fully implemented program would produce considerable economies of scale. For example, if a school had 15 apprentices and 3 academic teachers, the pupil-teacher ratio would be 5 to 1 (an expensive program on a per student basis). The same three teachers could serve more apprentices. For example, the teachers could team each 30 apprentices for 2 1/2 days a week while another 30 apprentices are at their worksites. AT midweek the first group goes tot their worksites, while the second group is in school for academic instruction. With a ratio of 20 students per teacher, this would be considerable less expensive in a per-pupil basis.

How Much Should Youth Apprentices Be Paid?

There are a number of perspectives on whether and how much youth apprentices should be paid. Some argue that apprentices should be paid a stipend (less than minimum wage) or even no wage at all. The argument is that the apprenticeship is part of the student's education. Offering a wage might attract students who are more interested in the money than in the educational value of the apprenticeship. Others point out that requiring participating businesses to pay at least minimum wage show business commitment to the program. They are more likely to take apprentices seriously and value their work if they pay them. Another perspective is that it is unrealistic not to pay youth apprentices. Apprenticeship programs will be competing against other jobs in the youth labor market. If the apprentices are not paid or paid less than high school students can earn elsewhere, programs may have problems filling positions as students opt for higher paying jobs. Federal ad State labor laws may influence what apprentices are paid. For example, one apprenticeship program began by requiring employers to pay a stipend ($2.00 per hour) rather than minimum wage ($4.25). Program administrators preferred the lower wage because they could point out to students that they were investing in their education by taking a lower salary. However, the State labor department has required that they receive minimum wage because the apprentices are "producing" products and services.[70]

Abuse of Young Workers

Concern has been raised that youth apprenticeships have the potential for exploitation of young workers. One concern is the health and safety of high school students, espe-

---

[70] The National Alliance of Business adivses: "IN general, youth apprentice employees shoudl be paid at the leve of their productivityu comapre with othter employees and in line iwth the demands of the labor market...If studnets are only particpating in job training classes, the don't necessarily have to be paid, If they are productive workers, then they sould be paid according to normal procedures...Ideally, there would be a series of clear pay increases granted as knowledge and skills are attained." National Alliance of Business, Real Jobs for Real People. p. 32.

cially those working in dangerous settings. Questions include who is liable if a student is injured on the job? Is it the the employer? Is it the school? Is the youth apprentice covered under workers' compensation?

Even if a youth apprentice is not working in a hazardous work environment, his or her well being could be jeopardized in other ways. For example, some research suggests that working longer than 15 or 20 hours per week can have a negative influence in high school students' academic achievement.[71] If students are attending school full time and working 30 or 40 hours a week, they may not get enough sleep; they will probably not have the time or energy to do homework; and extracurricular activities will likely be out of the question.[72]

One strategy for preventing abuse would be to require participants in a Federal youth apprentice program to agree to various assurances, including adherence to health and safety rules and limiting hours worked per week.[73] These assurances could be formalized for each apprentice in a written training agreement or contract signed by the school district's representatives, the employer, the parents, and the student. The agreement could lay out responsibilities and expectations for each party. For example, the student would agree to maintaining a specified grade point average, limit school and work absenteeism, and know and obey workplace safety rules. The school district might guarantee certain results such as high school graduation if the student upholds his or her responsibilities. The employer would agree to provide high quality job training in a safe environment.

SETTING UNIFORM OCCUPATIONAL STANDARDS

As noted above, a key aspect of a youth apprenticeship **system** is a process that certifies that those successfully completing the program have acquired skills in a particular occupation. But implementing such a system raises several policy questions about who should set standards and how standards should be set.

Some argue that teachers alone cannot set specific occupational standards because they do not know enough about the skill requirements of specific occupations. Others point out that business people cannot do it alone because they might set standards too narrowly to reflect specific skills in their plan (for example, skills required to operate specific milling machines that other plants do not have). Still others argue that business cannot be expected to set standards because they may not know what skills they need.[74] Another problem with skill standards and assessment is what the process may center on proficiencies in individual skills; whereas, what is really important is how well workers perform overall processes requiring many skills. "Knowing how to measure a part is a discrete skill. But being able to use that and other skills to work with a blueprint and

---

[71] Greenberger, Ellen ad Laurence Steinberg. When Teenagers Work. New York, Basic Books, 1986. p. 228.

[72] One apprenticeship program we visited tries to limit apprentices' work to 2 hours per day. Of course there is no way to keep studnets from working additianl jobs that are separate from the apprenticeship. There is some anecdotal evidence that some apprentices do this.

[73] For example of assurances, see S. 2745 intorduced durning the 102d Congress.

[74] One lesson gleaed form DOL's demonstatioon projects is that many participating employers are hving problemes becasue thtey have never before had to idnetify key worker skills, at least in the detail needed to revise curriculum and certify competence. Lessons Learned from School-to-Work Demonstration Projects, p. 2 [from DOL, but no author, date or agency attributin].

build a part using whatever tools, methods, or skills are necessary" is what really needs to be assessed.[75]

It is obvious that various "stakeholders" (e.g., business, unions, educational institutions, and government) must be involved in the standards-setting process, but just how is unclear. Lerman and Pouncy discuss one possible model: the Federal Institute for Vocational Training in Germany. This entity "is governed by a board drawn from employers, unions, and the government. Through the Institute, competency standards are developed for nearly 400 occupational areas, a process that often takes years of research and negotiation among the parties. The standards specify the minimum competencies for an occupation as well as a training plan that guides the timing, sequencing, and organization of the training. Regional chambers, made up of business and union representatives, govern the program at the local level. They check the suitability of firm training, organize exams, deal with complaints, provide technical assistance, help match trainees with training firms."[76]

ACCESS FOR MINORITIES AND WOMEN

Historically minorities and women have not had equal access to traditional apprenticeship programs, which raises concern that similar problems could arise in youth apprenticeships. While their participation rates in civilian apprenticeships have grown, problems of access apparently still exist.[77] For example, the General Accounting Office (GAO) found that, although minorities hold a proportion of apprenticeships roughly equal to their participation rate in the workforce, minority apprentices tend to cluster in programs for lower paying occupations and are underrepresented in those for higher paying occupations. Women's participation in apprenticeships does not approximate their rate of labor market participation; and like minorities they have less access to apprenticeships in higher paying occupations.[78]

To what extent should youth apprenticeships be targeted to "special" populations such as the disadvantaged and women? This question will take on increasing importance over the next decade because labor market projections indicate that new workers entering the workforce will increasingly be women and minorities. Population projections indicate that women could account for three f ever five "net additions" to the workforce between 1988 and 2000. (Net additions take into account workers entering and leaving the workforce.) Blacks could account for nearly 17 percent of net additions, and Hispanics should account for more than 27 percent. In addition, because of declining numbers of young workers, employers might need to hire many who, in the past, they ignored or avoided, such as the economically and educationally disadvantaged.[79]

[75] Jobs for the Future. New Training sTrategies for a High Performance Metalworking Industry. Report of a Conference. Cambridge, authror, 1991. p. 29.

[76] Lerman, Robert Il, and Hillary Pouncy. Why America Should Deveop a Youth Apprenticeshp System. Progress Policy Insitute Policy Report, no. 5, Mar. 1990. p.6.

[77] For an example of recent congressina ction, see OP.L. 102-530, the Women in Apprenticeshp and Nontraditional Occupations Act.

[78] Minorities hold approximately 22 percnet of all civilian apprentices; women hodl about 7 percnt. U.S. Genral Accounting Office. Apprenticeshp Training: Administration, Use,a d Equal Opportunity. Report to Congressional Rquresters GAO/HRD-92-43, Mar. 1992. Appendix I Wshington, Mar. 1992. p. 30-31.

[79] For futher discussion of these trneds, see U.S. Congress. Joint Economic Committee. Subcommittee on Techonology and Natinal Security. Demographic Change and the Economy of the Ninteties. Chapter III. Demography and the Labor Force in te 1990s. Reprot, S.Prt 1`02-55, 102 d Congress, 1st Session. Washington, GPO, 1991.

There appeared to be some consensus, at lest in the sites we visited, that youth apprenticeship programs should aim to serve the "middle 50 percent" of the high school population. Apprenticeships may benefit others such as the disabled and the students form families in severe poverty, both these groups have needs that apprenticeships alone could not fulfill.[80] Apprenticeships may also benefit the upper 25 percent - the college bound- but some argue that this group has other resources to draw from and should not have first priority for apprenticeships.[81] It is the middle group ("regular students" as one superintendent called them) that both can benefit from and need the services of youth apprenticeships.

CONCLUDING REMARKS

Arguably, youth apprenticeships have potential benefits for a large group of today's high school students. A well conceived and skillfully run program can help students improve academic achievement, acquire needed general and specific workforce training, complete high school, obtain postsecondary credentials, and ease the transition into the adult labor force. Carefully integrated academic instruction and on-the-job training can have beneficial effects to the students performance both in school and at work. Thoughtful supervision from a mentor or a job coach can teach specific job skills and socialize the student to he adult world.

At the same time, youth apprenticeships will not solve every problem that high school students face. Youth apprenticeships will not create jobs. Clearly, a youth apprenticeship program cannot even begin if the area it serves has lost many high paying, high skilled jobs. No matter how well trained youth apprentices are at the end of the program, if there are no high paying jobs available, they will face the same situation they would have faced had they obtained no training. In addition, youth apprenticeships may not be what every high school student needs. A youth apprenticeship program alone probably will be insufficient to greatly improve the prospects of students experiencing the sever disadvantages of growing up in areas of concentrated poverty.

Planning and implementing successful youth apprenticeship programs will be challenging. We have no precise model for these programs: Neither the European approaches nor American adult apprenticeships can be applied to American high school students without substantial modification. Inventing an American youth apprenticeship system will require breakthroughs on several fronts. These programs require more than just educational reform. They also hinge on serious involvement and commitment from employers, employees, and their representatives. not only will teachers need to revise what and how they teach, but workers must learn new roles in mentoring a coaching teenagers. Furthermore, the widespread implementation of youth apprenticeships will rest on national systems of occupational standards and certification. For students and employers to take these programs seriously, students must be able to certify their accomplishments when they complete their apprenticeship and see the benefit of participation and persistence.

---

[80] Some that we interviewed worry that, if the program is too expllicity targeted on the disadvantaged, it will be seen as a "dumping gournd," just as vocaitonal education often is. AS a result, "better" studnets my be more difficutl to recruit, and emplyers may be less likely to participate.

[81] At leas some of the teachers and business leaders we talked with belive that haveing som "A" studnets adds to the prestige of the program and removes the stigma some attach to vocational education.

Finally, it is unclear what the Federal role should be in creating and fostering youth apprenticeships. Should that role be limited to technical assistance and research, allowing States, local governments, and the private sector to decide how much this country invests in youth apprenticeships? Should the Federal Government assume more leadership but at a relatively slow pace - investing Federal resources first n demonstrations and planning before making a decision for or against a nationwide program? Or should the Federal Government take advantage of what some see as an infrequently occurring "window of opportunity" for a national initiative and authorize a nationwide youth apprenticeship program - hoping to work out problems and improve the program over time?

PARTICIPATION REQUIREMENTS
IN THE JOB OPPORTUNITIES
AND BASIC SKILLS (JOBS) PROGRAM:
HOW DO THEY WORK?

Carmen D. Solomon

SUMMARY

The Family Support Act of 1988 (P.L. 100-485) specifies that a certain percentage of recipients of the program of Aid to Families with Dependent Children (AFDC) must participate in a work, education, or training activity in order for the State to receive "enhanced" matching funds for the Federal Government. Federal matching rates for States that meet participation standards range for 60 to 79 percent, compared to a flat 50 percent rate for States that fail. According to the Act, 15 percent of all persons not exempt for participation in the AFDC education, work, and training program, called Job Opportunities and Basic Skills (JOBS), must actually be JOBS participants in FY 1994 (up from 11 percent in FY 1992-19930> In addition, the law imposes special JOBS participation requirements on AFDC-Unemployment Parent (UP) families in FY 1994. Ultimately (in FY 1997 ad FY 1998) at least one of the tow parents in 75 percent of all AFDC-UP families must work at least 16 hours per week in a specified work activity.

There is widespread disagreement about the level of the federal participation requirements, the manner of measurement, and the reliability of State participation data. Concern that the FY 1994 participation rates for AFDC-UP families might cause some States to scale back their programs by focusing on job search and placement activities led the House Ways and Means Committee to propose a 1-year delay in their start. The House accepted this change as a provision of the Omnibus Budget Reconciliation Act of 1993 (P.L. 101-66), but Senate conferees rejected it.

BACKGROUND

GENERAL

Since October 1, 1990, States have been required (to the extent resources are available) to require nonexempt recipients of AFDC to participate in JOBS. The JOBS program provides education, work and training to AFDC recipients. Its purposes is to help individuals avoid long-term welfare dependency.[1] Under JOBS, AFDC recipients with children under age 13 cannot be required to enroll in JOBS unless child care is "guaranteed". In addition, JOBS participants must be reimbursed for transportation expenses. Nonexempt AFDC recipients who refuse without good cause to (1) participate in the JOBS program or (2) accept any bona fide offer of employment must be sanctioned. If an individual is sanctioned, the law requires that this or her needs be ignored in determining the family's AFDC benefit; thus, the family's income is reduces. In an AFDC-Up family, both parents must be sanctioned unless the second parent is participating in the JOBS program. AFDC applicants and recipients who are exempt form JOBS may participate voluntarily.[2] To assure that enhanced Federal matching funds are directed largely towards those most in need of assistance, the Family Support Act defines target groups and penalizes States by reducing Federal matching funds if a State does not spend at least 55 percent of its JOBS funds on them.[3]

The JOBS program is a "capped" entitlement. The law stipulates that States are "entitled" to a share f the JOBS funds appropriated each year. State allotments are based primarily in each States' share of the average monthly number of adult AFDC recipients in the Nation. congress has appropriated the full JOBS authorization for each fiscal year to date. To "draw down" the funds appropriated for JOBS, States must provide matching funds. In FY 1992, because of tight State budgets, only 65 percent ($655 million) of the $1 billion in Federal funds appropriated for JOBS was claimed by the States.

JOBS Authorization	
FY 1989	$600 million
FY 1990	$800 million
FY 1991-1993	$1.0 billion
FY 1994	$1.1 billion
FY 1995	$1.3 billion
FY 1996 & later	$1.0 billion

PARTICIPATION REQUIREMENTS

During consideration of the Family Support Act, the Senate was adamant about requiring States to engage significant proportions of their AFDC caseloads in the JOBS program. The Senate's concern stemmed from the low participation levels recorded in the Work Incentive (WIN) program, predecessor to JOBS. Because WIN had limited funding and the law's sanction applied only to failure to register a specified fraction of AFDC

---

[1] The Family Support Act exempts AFDC recipients who are employed 30 or more house per week for JOBS participation requirements. Under the regulations, persons who are employed for less than 30 hours per week usually do not count as JOBS participants unless theya re enrolled in other counted activities. In light of recent studies showing much movement between work an dwelfare, some obsrvers say that the JOBS program should focus more on retainig employment. Hence, they maintain that recipients who work part-time should be counted as JOBS participants.

[2] Exempt for JOBS are (1) persons who are ill, incpacitated, or of advanced age; (2) children under age 16; (3) children between ages 16 and 18 (or 19, at State option) who are attending full time an elementary or secondary school or who are enrolled in a vocatinal or technical prgram full time; (4) parents or other relative caretakers of a child under age 3 who are personally prviding care for the child; (5) parents or other relative caretakers of a child between 3 and 6, unless child care is "guaranteed" (requred particpation cannot exceed 20 hours per week); (6) persons whose presence in the home is required because of the illenss or incpapacity of another household member; (7) persons working 30 hours or more a week; (10) pregnant women in their second or third trimest; and (11) persons living in areas where the program is not available.

[3] The target groups are (1) persons who have received AFDC for any 36 of the preceding 60 months; (2) applicants who ahve recieved AFDS for any 36 of the 60 months immediately preceding application; (3) custodial parents under age 24 who have not completed high school and are not enrolled in high school (or equivalent) or who have lttle or no work experience in the preceding year; and (4) members of a family inwhich the youngest child is withing 2 years of being ineligible for AFDC because of age.

recipients, the program in many areas was essentially a "paper" process. Many Senate members held the view that WIN's lack of actual participation rules had cost the program its credibility. The Senate added workprogram participation standards, reinforced by loss of some Federal funds, to the bill that became the Family Support Act.

Under the Act, minimum participation requirements were established for FY 1990-1995. Theses general participation require-ments expire on October 1, 1995. If a State does not meet annual participation rates, its Federal matching funds are to be reduced to 50 percent. In addition, beginning in FY 1994, in order for a State to receive enhanced JOBS

JOBS: Required Participation Rates		
General	*AFDC-UP*	
FY 1990-1991: 7%	FY 1994:	40%
FY 1992-1993: 11%	FY 1995:	50%
FY 1994: 15%	FY 1996:	60%
FY 1995: 20%	FY 1997-1998:	75%

funding,[4] it must have a specified percentage of its AFDC-UP caseload engaged in work activities for at least 16 hours per week.[5] These AFDC-UP participation rate requirements expire October 1, 1998. The Omnibus Budget Reconciliation Act of 1993 dropped a House-passed provision that would have delayed imposition of AFDC-UP participation rates by 1 year. Federal welfare officials have indicated that they will issue special guidance on implementing the 40 percent participation requirement.

HOW IS PARTICIPATION MEASURED?

The Family Support Act gave the Secretary of DHHS the responsibility of defining "participation". The Family Support Act also requires the DHHS Secretary to develop performance standards. The law says that these standards must be measured by out-come and not solely by levels of activity or participation. Federal regulations stipulate that participation will be measured in terms of a 20-hour-per-week standard. Under this rule, the welfare agency is instructed to count as participants the largest number of per-sons whose combined and averaged hours during the month equal 20. This means that if one person is in an adult basic education course that is scheduled for 15 hours per week, another person would have to be in a component that required 25 hours per week of attendance in order for both to be counted toward the 20-hour-per-week standard. This does not mean that four individuals participating for 15 hours a week would be counted as three participants. In fact, those four individuals would represent zero par-ticipants, since no group of persons averaged 20 hours per week. Further, the welfare agency must verify that the individual attended at lest 75 percent of the hors scheduled for the month. Otherwise, participation is counted as zero even if the actual hours of attendance exceeded 20 hours per week. Thus, if an individual is enrolled in a JOBS ac-tivity during the middle of the month, it is unlikely that he or she will meet the 75-percent test; hence, the State could not count that person as a JOBS participant. Roughly speaking, in calculating the participation rate percentage, the numerator is the number

---

[4] The Federal enhnced matching rate for JOBS activities, including costs of full-time personeel, ranges from 60 to 79 percent among the States, with rates inversely related to per capia income. The Federal matching rate for a State must be reduced to 50 percent if: (1) It does spend at least 55 percent of its JOBS funds on taraget groups, (2) it fails to meet general participation rate requriements, or (3) it fails to meet the special particpation re-quirements of AFDC-Up families. (JOBS administrative costs are matched at a rate of 50 percent; transportation and supportive services, excluding chld care, also are matched at 50 percent; and child care costs, funded sepa-rately, are amtched at a rate that varies among States form 50-79 percent.)

[5] Work activities include work supplementatin, community work experience (CWEP) or other work experinece program, on-the-job training, or a State-desinged work prgram approved by the Secratry of DHHS. States may require parents under age 25 who do have not completed high school or an equivalent course of study to engage in schooling instead of these work programs.

of persons who meet both the 20-hour rule and the 75-percent test and the denominator is the number of nonexempt adult AFDC recipients.

In determining whether recipients meet the 20-hour rule, a State would exclude individuals who have not met the 75-percent test; arrange those who are participating satisfactorily in rank order with those with most hours at the top; and then calculate a running or cumulative average. Individuals remaining once the average drops below 20 would not be counted as participants. In the following example only three recipients would be considered JOBS participants.

Number of Individuals	Weekly hours of participation	Average # of hours per week
1	24	24.00
2	20	22.00
3	20	21.33
4	15	19.75

GAO REPORTS THAT STATES ARE NOT MEASURING PARTICIPATION ACCURATELY

According to the General Accounting Office (GAO): DHHS is making decisions related to providing states millions of dollars in federal JOBS funds that are based upon inaccurate state-reported participation rate data. These data are not comparable derived across states and should not be relied upon by policymakers as a basis for comparing states' performance.[6] GAO says that States have deviated from the JOBS regulations in whom they count as required to participate, what activities they count toward hours of participation, whom they determine to have met the attendance requirement, and whom they count as participants.

EXPERIENCE TO DATE

JOBS DATA

In FY 1992, there was 4.4 million adult AFDC recipients, of whom 2.5 million were exempt form JOBS participation. In FY 1992, 310,754 was the average monthly number of persons counted as JOBS "participants". As indicated earlier, the number of AFDC recipients who actually engaged in a JOBS activity was greater than 310,754 because not all of them met the rules to count as a participant.

In FY 1992, 4 jurisdictions (Guam, Indiana, Maine, and Maryland) failed to meet the 11 percent JOBS participation requirement.[7] The JOBS participation rates for FY 1992 ranged from 3.8 percent in Guam to 77 percent in Nebraska. California, which had an AFDC adult population of 705,000, had a FY 1992 JOBS participation rate of 12.3 percent. New York, which had an AFDC adult population of 374,000, had a JOBS participation rate of 15.1 percent.

---

[6] U.S. General Accounting Office. Welfare to Work: JOBS Particpation Rate Data Unreliable for Assessing States' Performance. May 1993. GO/HRD-93-73. p.12.

[7] The JOBS participation rate for FY 1992 was 3.8 percent in Guam, 6.6 percent in Indiana, 9.5 percent in Maine, and 10.5 percent in Maryland.

"MAXIMUM" FEASIBLE PARTICIPATION RATES -PAST EXPERIENCE.

The San Diego County Saturation Work Initiative Model (SWIM) sought to achieve a 75 percent participation rate for nonexempt AFDC recipients. The Manpower Demonstration Research Corporation (MDRC) evaluation[8] of SWIM found that during its second year (1986, pro-JOBS), monthly participation rates averaged 22 percent if only program-arranged services were counted, increased to 33 percent when education and training activities initiated by recipients were added, and reached 52 percent if employment that occurred while individual were still registered with the program were included.[9] These relatively low rates were achieved by using a very liberal definition of participation, excluding mothers with children under age 6 from work requirements, and close monitoring and intensive counseling by caseworkers.

Although the actual participation rates fell far short of the 75 percent saturation goal, MDRC found that close to 90 percent of individuals eligible for SWIM services in any month were engaged in a program activity or had a legitimate excuse for not being active.

A study of Ohio's pre-JOBS (1983-1985) community work experience program,[10] in which recipients worked in exchange for their AFDC benefits, found that approximately 25 percent of all adult AFDC recipients (including families with very young children) and over 80 percent of AFDC-UP recipients in the demonstration counties participated in the AFDC work program.

For JOBS to achieve a 50 percent participation rate (of nonexempt persons) - somewhat like that of San Diego, or a 25 percent rate (of all adult recipients) - like that of Ohio, roughly 1 million persons monthly would have to be JOBS participants.[11]

ISSUES

ADMINISTRATIVE BURDEN

There is widespread agreement among JOBS administrators that meeting future participation standards may be a major problem. Many have indicated that their difficulty is not with the law itself, but rather with the way in which the Federal regulations have interpreted the law. Some find the participation standards as delineated in the Federal regulations to be unreasonable and unworkable.[12] Under current rules, administrators must keep tack of each individual's participation hours and must verify via a sampling

---

[8] Hamilton, Gayle. *Interim Report on the Saturation Work Initiative Model in San Diego.* Manpwoer Demonstration Research Corporation. Aug. 1988. See also: Hamilton, Gayle and Daniel Friedlander. *Final Report on the Saturation Work Initiative Model in San Diego.* Nov. 1989.

[9] The SWIM program used a very liberal definition of particpation. The denominator of th eprticipation rate was the nubmer of individuals who had attended a program orientation and were eligivle for the program at least 1 day during a given month. The numberator was the number of individuals who were active for at least 1 hour during a given month in job search, work experience, education, training, or part-time employment.

[10] Schiller, Bradley R., and C. Nielsen Brasher. Effects of Workfare Saturation on AFDC Caseloads. *Contemporary Policy Issues,* v. XI, Jan. or Apr. 1993.

[11] San Diego particpation rate = 50% x 1.9 million adults requred to aprticpate in JOBS = 950,000. Ohio rate = 25% x 4.4 million adult AFDC recipients = 1.1 million.

[12] The 102d Congress passed legislation that wllowed each hour of classroom training offered at a postsecondary instituion to be cunted as 2 hours of aprticpation in JOBS. However, that provision died with the pocket veto of the tax bill.

of cases whether participants attend a JOBS component for at least 75 percent of the scheduled monthly hours. They argue that this requires so much staff time that it may result in a less effective program. In part, the tracking problems exist because most States are operating ht JOBS program with less than fully automated systems.[13]

GAO found that some States have not been calculating their JOBS participation rates in accordance with Federal regulations and DHHS detailed directives.

APPROPRIATENESS OF PRESENT RATE LEVELS

Some observers argue that participation rates should be close to 100 percent, since the rates apply only to persons expected to participate, i.e., those not exempt. State officials have testified that philosophically their goal is to enroll all able-bodied nonexempt AFDC recipients in JOBs, and some have said participation rates would rise if Federal funding were higher. S. 16, sponsored by Finance Committee chairman Danile P. Moynihan, would remove the Federal funding cap and increase the general AFDC participation rate form 15 percent in FY 1994 to 50 percent. Some proponents of high participation rates say these are needed to induce AFDC recipients to change their expectations and behaviors (e.g., successfully complete training programs, find jobs, view AFDC as a temporary means of support).
One of the conclusions of the MDRC evaluation that localities will face unequal challenges in trying to achieve the same numerical participation rates because of factors such as the job market, the extent to which States allow individuals to use self-initiated education and training, the rates of turnover in the AFDC program, and the employability of recipients.

POSSIBLE POLICY EFFECTS OF 1994 AFDC-UP RATES

Many administrators have testified that the 40 percent participation rate for AFDC-UP families scheduled to go into effect beginning in FY 1994 may cause States to (1) change the focus of their JOBS programs from educational activities to job search activities, (2) divert funds from the target groups to the AFDC-UP caseload (who may or may not be in the target groups), and (3) be less sensitive to the needs and problems of recipients. Moreover, even with these policy changes, some States might not meet the higher JOBS participation rates.

However, some States might not even attempt to meet the new participation rates. Some might conclude that they would save money by accepting the lower 50 percent Federal matching rate, because the "enhanced" Federal matching rate wouldn't offset the extra State costs of expanding the JOBS program enough to meet the participation rules.

---

[13] The MDRC report stated that States without an automated tracking system were at a disadvantage because welfare staff had to manually examine case file data. Even with a very good SWIM automated tracking syste, the MDRC report stated that county staff spend substantial time ensuring the accuracy and completeness of the data.

THE JOB OPPORTUNITIES AND BASIC SKILLS (JOBS) PROGRAM

Gene Falk
Education and Public Welfare Division

SUMMARY

The Job Opportunities and Basic Skills (JOBS) program, enacted by the Family Support Act of 1988 (P.L. 100-485), provides education and training to recipients of Aid to Families with Dependent Children (AFDC). Each State runs it own program within Federal rules and guidelines. The Federal Government reimburses States for a share of spending in their program, though there are national and State caps on Federal JOBS funding. Since the program took effect nationwide in Fiscal Year (FY) 1991, Federal JOBS grants (including grants of Indian tribes) have grown from $684 million to $873 million in FY 1994 cap of $1.1 billion; 19 States reached their maximum Federal grant in FY 1994.

FEDERAL-STATE FINANCING OF JOBS

The Federal Government reimburses States for a share of their expenditures in their JOBS programs, which provides education and employment training for recipients of AFDC. The Federal reimbursement rate for JOBS expenditures varies by State. The JOBS reimbursement rate, to a large extent, is inversely related to State per-capita income, and varies from 60% I the highest income State to a maximum of 80%. States that fail too meet participation requirements have their reimbursement rate reduced to 50%. Additionally, a 50% reimbursement rate applies to administrative expenses other than full-time personnel and for work-related expenses other than child care (separately funded). Federal reimbursements for JOBS are capped. In FY1994, the national cap was $1.1 billion. In FY1995, the national cap on JOBS funding is $1.3 billion. For FY1996 and subsequent years, the JOBS caps falls to $1.0 billion. Each State is provided an "allotment," which represents its share of the national cap and limits Federal payments to the State for JOBS. Allotments are made based on each State's share of the national total number of adult AFDC recipients. More than 80 Indian tribes and Alaska Native Organizations have chosen to operate their own JOBS programs, independent of their State. Allotments to Indian tribes reduce a State's JOBS allotment. Indian JOBS funds are 100% federally paid.

FINANCIAL TRENDS IN THE JOBS PROGRAM

The JOBS program was enacted in 1988. Some States began JOBS programs in FY1989, though States were not required to operate a program until FY1991. Federal grants to States for JOBS increased 28% from FY1991 to FY1994, reflecting increased State expenditures for JOBS. In FY1991, total JOBS grants were $684 million, 68% of the national cap. The JOBS grant increased to $873 million, 79% of the national cap, in FY1994.

Chart 1 shows the JOBS cap and grant from FY1989 the first year the program could operate) to FY1994. The program began nationwide operation in FY1991.

CHART 1. JOBS CAP and JOBS GRANT
FY1989-FY1994

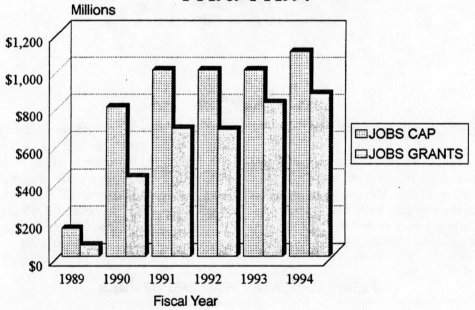

Source: Chart prepared by the Congressional Research Service (CRS)
based on data from the U.S. Department of Health and Human Services, 5/95.

The number of States at the JOBS cap increased substantially between FY1992 and FY1993. IN FY1992, only nine States took full advantage of Federal funding for JOBS. In FY1993, 20 States were at the JOBS cap. This number declined to 19 States in FY1994, when the JOBS cap was raised by 10%. Table 1 shows State JOBS grants as a percent of their JOBS ceilings

Table 1 JOBS Grant as a Percent of JOBS Cap by State,
FY 1991-FY1994

State	1991	1992	1993	1994
Alabama	47.28	80.35	100.00	100.00
Alaska	99.96	91.92	100.00	100.00
Arizona	78.37	53.38	63.17	70.88
Arkansas	100.00	100.00	100.00	99.99
California	72.34	64.70	87.22	75.01
Colorado	57.31	58.47	73.94	73.35
Connecticut	96.56	71.33	59.68	58.20
Delaware	98.50	100.00	96.91	100.00
District of Columbia	71.06	71.49	91.46	85.18
Florida	49.67	46.95	44.64	36.05
Georgia	53.07	48.07	65.84	74.22
Guam	100.00	83.63	88.12	70.33
Hawaii	91.06	88.97	100.00	100.00
Idaho	100.00	100.00	100.00	100.00
Illinois	45.94	39.96	52.76	59.43
Indiana	72.13	48.71	67.19	67.11
Iowa	71.21	61.24	71.48	100.00
Kansas	61.81	73.15	100.00	96.32
Kentucky	9.47	76.92	83.94	84.18
Louisiana	86.60	75.96	100.00	100.00
Maine	86.58	48.48	66.75	51.00
Maryland	99.47	100.00	84.34	91.59
Massachusetts	85.67	80.63	84.04	71.01
Michigan	45.00	45.58	100.00	100.00
Minnesota	76.52	66.09	86.57	88.74
Mississippi	46.97	27.88	100.00	100.00
Missouri	34.44	31.60	53.22	55.69
Montana	83.53	99.99	100.00	78.92
Nebraska	57.73	99.25	95.45	67.78
Nevada	29.78	58.06	68.16	51.22
New Hampshire	100.00	100.00	100.00	100.00
New Jersey	100.00	89.23	100.00	93.99
New Mexico	49.84	23.82	23.64	25.76
New York	77.83	92.06	100.00	100.00
North Carolina	77.02	76.10	84.82	81.51
North Dakota	100.00	100.00	76.43	100.00
Ohio	74.06	82.64	79.56	88.31
Oklahoma	83.58	65.27	100.00	75.41
Oregon	100.00	100.00	100.00	100.00
Pennsylvania	65.80	82.25	94.11	100.00
Puerto Rico	28.63	59.16	88.83	81.53
Rhode Island	98.09	84.22	88.15	98.63
South Carolina	67.08	40.72	56.18	52.45
South Dakota	67.93	97.19	100.00	100.00

<h4 style="text-align:center">Table 1 (Continued)</h4>

Tennessee	20.34	38.54	27.23	27.24
Texas	57.22	55.55	81.80	67.86
Utah	75.59	82.39	100.00	100.00
Vermont	84.48	60.79	100.00	100.00
Virgin Islands	100.00	100.00	100.00	100.00
Virginia	82.43	83.28	59.36	73.59
Washington	43.88	60.54	83.36	66.94
West Virginia	68.62	82.39	92.63	79.97
Wisconsin	100.00	100.00	100.00	100.00
Wyoming	100.00	100.00	96.80	100.00
Number of States at the cap	10	9	20	19

Note: These percentages are rounded. In a few cases (for example, New York in FY1994), a State is slightly below the JOBS cap but the rounded percentage is 100%.

Source: Table prepared by the Congressional Research Service (CRS) based on data from the U.S. Department of Health and Human Services (DHHS), May 1995.

FINANCING JOBS PROGRAMS BY STATE, FY1994

In FY1994, the total JOBS grant was $873 million. Under Federal regulations, States have 2 years to liquidate (expend) obligations made under the JOBS programs. Therefore, States have through Sept. 30, 1995 to expend all of their FY1994 JOBS funds.

Table 2. Federal Funding and the Federal Share, State Share, and Total JOBS Expenditures, FY1994 ($ in thousands)

State	Federal JOBS funding			FY 1994 expenditures (through 5/95)	
	JOBS allocation	JOBS grants	Federal share of expenditures	State share of expenditures	Total expenditures
Alabama	9,544	9,544	9,544	3,851	13,394
Alaska	2,104	2,104	2,104	1,387	3,490
Arizona	12,748	9,036	7,000	4,159	11,160
Arkansas	5,144	5,143	4,999	3,879	8,878
California	177,014	132,784	108,288	79,885	188,172
Colorado	10,906	7,999	9,056	5,160	14,216
Connecticut	13,086	7,616	9,190	5,908	15,098
Delaware	2,333	2,333	2,193	1,372	3,566
District of Columbia	5,556	4,733	5,190	2,841	8,031
Florida	48,488	17,482	12,741	14,007	26,748
Georgia	27,858	20,677	16,841	11,402	28,243
Guam	452	318	195	85	280
Hawaii	4,674	4,674	4,674	7,374	12,048
Idaho	2,552	2,552	2,552	1,587	4,139
Illinois	51,974	30,887	30,563	20,295	50,858
Indiana	16,693	11,202	10,769	7,419	18,188
Iowa	8,741	8,741	8,741	5,393	14,134

Table 2 (Continued)

Kansas	7,001	6,743	6,214	4,105	10,319
Kentucky	18,189	15,314	13,245	8,638	21,884
Louisiana	16,607	16,607	16,607	14,894	31,502
Maine	6,076	3,099	5,627	4,236	9,862
Maryland	17,498	16,027	13,119	8,300	21,419
Massachusetts	28,836	20,476	22,366	13,510	35,876
Michigan	59,316	59,316	42,122	26,755	68,877
Minnesota	15,445	13,706	13,313	8,110	21,423
Mississippi	10,977	10,977	5,534	3,277	8,810
Missouri	20,844	11,609	11,527	7,739	19,266
Montana	2,769	2,185	2,459	1,052	3,511
Nebraska	3,650	2,474	2,653	1,622	4,275
Nevada	2,626	1,345	1,142	700	1,842
New Hampshire	2,528	2,528	3,481	2,785	6,265
New Jersey	28,297	26,596	28,297	18,334	46,631
New Mexico	6,852	1,765	1,992	983	2,974
New York	98,421	98,418	87,799	62,540	150,340
North Carolina	25,228	20,564	20,665	14,478	35,143
North Dakota	1,458	1,458	853	239	1,092
Ohio	58933	52,046	52,245	41,939	94,183
Oklahoma	9,861	7,437	7,322	383	11,125
Oregon	11892	11,892	11,892	7,099	18,992
Pennsylvania	47,968	47,968	37,633	26,267	63,900
Puerto Rico	13,563	11,059	7,156	3,253	10,409
Rhode Island	5,211	5,140	4,588	3,070	7,657
South Carolina	9,549	5,008	6,099	2,586	8,685
South Dakota	1,251	1,251	1,242	518	1,760
Tennessee	21,110	5,750	8,941	4,879	13,820
Texas	52,507	35,634	35,812	23,305	59,116
Utah	4,796	4,796	4,796	1,757	6,553
Vermont	3,273	3,273	3,172	1,865	5,037
Virgin Islands	339	339	286	105	391
Virginia	14,676	10,800	10,294	7,226	17,520
Washington	26,285	17,595	16,329	8,790	25,119
West Virginia	11,252	8,998	8,667	4,061	12,728
Wisconsin	25,780	25,780	23,974	14,928	38,902
Wyoming	1,544	1,544	1,457	1,068	2,525
Indian Programs	7,638	7,638			
Totals	1,099,910	872,978	785,559	534,819	1,320,378

Through May 1995, States reported expending a total of $1.3 billion on JOBS. The Federal share (financed through the FY1994 Federal JOBS grant) of this amount was $786 million. States spent from their own funds %535 million on JOBS. Table 2 shows FY1994 Federal JOBS funding and expenditures by State. The second and third columns on the tale provide FY1994 Federal funding: the JOBS cap applicable to the State (the "allocation") and the grant amount (Federal funding for JOBS activities for FY1994). In cases where States have drawn the full JOBS grant, columns 2 and 3 are identical. The fourth through sixth columns provide the FY1994 amounts expended through May 1995 on JOBS, dividing it among the Federal share and State share of expenditures base on FY1994 funding. Because States may continue to expend FY1994 moneys until the end of FY1995, these expenditure figures are likely to change. For those States where columns 3 and 4 are identical, all FY1994 JOBS funds have been expended.

TRAINING FOR DISLOCATED WORKERS UNDER THE JOB TRAINING PARTNERSHIP ACT

Ann Lordeman

SUMMARY

Employment and training assistance for dislocated workers is authorized by title III of the Job Training Partnership act (JTPA). Dislocated workers are generally characterized as workers with an established work history who have lost their jobs as a result of structural changes in the economy and who are not likely to find new jobs in their former industries or occupations.

Title III consists of four programs. For the most part, all four programs provide similar services; they differ primarily in the groups of dislocated workers who are eligible to receive services. The largest program is a "generic" program to assist workers regardless of the cause of the dislocation. This program, firs authorized in 1982, is funded at $516.6 million for FY1993. For the program year ending Junco 30, 1991, 107,500 persons participated in the program.

Three programs for specific groups of dislocated workers were created between 1990 and 1992 in response to changes in Federal policies that could result in worker dislocation. There was concern that without separate programs, these workers June have to compete with all dislocated workers for services, and therefore might not receive adequate assistance, The Defense Conversion Adjustment (DCA) program was created for workers dislocated as a result of cuts in defense spending or by base closures. Funded at $!50 million in FY1991, funds for this program are available through September 1997. The Clean Air Employment Transition Assistance program (CAETA), funded at $50 million for FY1993, was created for workers dislocated as a result of compliance with the Clean Air Act. The Defense Diversification program was created for certain members of the armed forces, certain defense employees, and certain defense contractor employees. It appears that the Secretary of Defense may expend $75 million in FY1993 funds for this program.

Currently, changes in international trade, technology, and public policies are resulting in increased concern about the plight of dislocated workers. Specifically, approval and implementation of the North America Free Trade Agreement (NAFTA) in 1993 could lead to job losses in some industries. Also, changing technologies may place new demands on worker skills that require retraining. Finally, with the end of the Cold War,

U.S. budget outlays for national defense are being cut significantly, resulting in job loss because of base closures and defense industry downsizing.

As the 103d Congress addresses the training needs of dislocated workers, it will most likely look to both the generic program an to the three programs targeted to certain groups of dislocated workers as potential models for new or revised dislocated worker programs.

INTRODUCTION

Dislocated workers are generally characterized as workers with an established work history who have lost their jobs as a result of structural changes in the economy and who are not likely to find new jobs in their former industries or occupations.[1] Currently, changes in international trade, technology and public policies are resulting in increased concern about the plight of dislocated workers. Specifically, approval and implementation of the North America Free Trade Agreement (NAFTA) in 1993 could lead to job losses in some industries. Also, changing technologies may place new demands on worker skills that require retraining. Finally, with the end of the cold War, U.S. budget outlays for national defense are being cut significantly, resulting in job loss because of base closures and defense industry downsizing.

There are two Federal statutes that authorize training specifically for workers dislocated as a result of these and other events: The Job Training Partnership Act (JTPA), which authorizes the title II dislocated worker program, and the Trade Act of 1962 which authorizes the Trade Adjustment Assistance (TAA) program. Title III primarily provides services t workers who lose their jobs regardless of the cause of the dislocation. On the other hand, TAA provides services only to workers who lose their jobs as a result of competition from imported goods. This report will focus on title Iii of JTPA.[2]

Title III consists of four programs, the largest of which is a "generic" program (i.e., it assists workers regardless of the cause of the dislocation). Title II also consists of three programs that serve specific groups of dislocated workers: the Defense Conversion Adjustment (DCA) program for workers dislocated as a result of cuts in defense spending or by base closures; the Defense Diversification program for certain members of the armed forces, certain defense employees, and certain defense contractor employees; and the Clean Air Employment Transition Assistance program (CAETA) for workers dislocated as a result of compliance with the Clean Air Act. For the most part the four programs provide similar services; they differ primarily in the groups of dislocated workers who are eligible to receive services.

As the 103d Congress addresses the training needs of dislocated workers, it will most likely look to both the generic program and to the programs targeted to certain groups of dislocated workers as potential models for new or revised dislocated worker programs. This report describes the generic program and the three specific program, with particular emphasis on allocation of funds, eligibility requirements for receiving services, and types of assistance available.

---

[1] For more information on dislocated workers, see: U.S. Library of Congress. Congressional Research Services. Dislocated Workers: Characteristics and Experiences, 1979-1992. CRS Report for Congress No 92-813 E, by Linda Levine. Washington, Nov. 16, 1992.

[2] For more information on TAA, see: U.S. Library of Congress. Congressional Research Service. Trade Adjustmetn Assistance: The Program for Workers. CRS Report for congress No. 92-73 EPW, by James R. Storey. Washington, Dec. 26, 1991.

BACKGROUND

The Manpower Development and Training Act of 1962 was one of the earliest post-World War II job training programs, and initially focused on experienced workers displaced due to automation. However, as unemployment rates began to fall among white males, the employment and training needs of minorities, youth, and the economically disadvantaged moved closer to the forefront. The Economic Opportunity Act of 1964 and the Comprehensive Employment and Training Act (CETA) of 1973 continued the emphasis in Federal job training policy on serving economically disadvantaged individuals with little prior work experience and low skill and education levels.

When the Job Training Partnership Act (JTPA) replaced CETA in 1982, unemployment was rising among experienced workers displaced from relatively high-wage jobs in declining industries. Under title III of the Act, Congress created a new program authorizing training and related services for dislocated workers who are permanently displaced from their jobs but who are not necessarily poor or unskilled.[3] The intent of this new generic program was to serve dislocated workers regardless of the cause of dislocation.

Unlike the larger JTPA program for the disadvantaged, in which Federal funds are passed through from the State to the local level, title III was originally established as a primarily State program. Seventy-five percent of the funds were distributed to States by a formula, and 25 percent were retained by the Secretary of Labor for national activities including a discretionary grant program.[4] There was, however, no formula or guidance for distributing funds within each State. Local agencies could review State title III plans but ultimate decisionmaking authority on how services would be delivered rested with the States.

In 1986, Congress made minor changes in JTPA including some minor changes to the title III program. In 1988, Congress completely revamped the title III program to address several criticisms of the program:

- slowness in responding to plant closings and layoffs;
- lack of a mechanism for encouraging cooperation among management, labor, and government in providing services to dislocated workers;
- failure to fully spend the funds allocated by Congress;
- the small percentage of dislocated workers receiving services;
- the limited amount of occupational training provided dislocated workers, and
- the failure of matching requirements to generate new cash of in-kind resources

The program was amended by the Omnibus Trade and Competitiveness Act of 1988 (P.L. 100-418), which included the Economic Dislocation and Worker Adjustment Assistance Act (EDWAA). Major changes included:

---

[3] Other programs uthroized under JTPA include training for low-income adults and youth, summer employment and training for low-income youngsters, the residential Job Corps program for severely disadvantaged youth, and programs for special popultion groups such as Native Americans, migrants and seasonal farmworkers, and veterans.

[4] Amendments to JTPA in 1988 increased the proportion of funds distributed to States to 80 o percent and decreased the proportion retained by the Secretary to 20 percent.

- the requirement that States establish dislocated worker units to respond rapidly to permanent closures and substantial layoffs;

- the requirement that State dislocated worker units promote the development of labor-management committees at the site of worker dislocation to develop strategies to deal with the employment and training needs of affected workers;

- provisions for the reallotment of unexpended funds to other States;

- the requirement that States distribute at least 60 percent of the funds to substate areas: 50 percent on the basis of a formula and 10 percent on a discretionary basis;

- the requirement that at least 50 percent of funds in a substate area be spent on retraining services, and

- elimination of the federal matching requirement.

Beginning in 1990, Congress amended title Iii to create new programs for specific groups of dislocated workers. These programs were created in response to changes in Federal policies that could result in worker dislocation. There was concern that without separate program, these workers would have to compete with all dislocated workers for services, and therefore might not receive adequate assistance. Specifically, the Clean Air Act Amendments of 1990 (P.L. 101-549) amended title II to include a CAETA program for workers dislocated as a result of compliance with the Clean Air Act. The National Defense Authorization Act for FY 1991 (P.L. 101-510) amended title III to include a Defense Conversion Assistance (DCA) program for workers dislocated as a result of reductions in defense spending.

In 1992, Congress again amended title III to create a third program for specific groups of dislocated workers. The National Defense Authorization Act for FY 1993 (P.L. 102-484) created a Defense Diversification program for certain discharged military personnel, terminated defense employees, ad displaced employees of defense contractors. From funds appropriated by the National Defense Appropriations Act, 1993, (P.L. 102-396), it appears that the Secretary of Defense may be authorized to fund this new program, which would be administered by the Secretary of Labor. As of now, it is unclear whether appropriations will be used to fund the program.

The National Defense Authorization Act for FY 1993 also made amendments to the generic program and to the DCA program. These amendments make it possible for workers to being receiving services once an announcement has been ma e that a facility is closing rather than waiting to receive an actual notice of termination. Other amendments were made to ensure that States deliver services rapidly to dislocated workers. Also in 1992, very limited changes were made specifically to title III when Congress passed amendments to other titles of JTPA (P.L. 102-367) to increase targeting to very disadvantaged individuals and to strengthen it s fiscal integrity.

AUTHORIZATIONS

Generic program. The generic program is permanently authorized by title III of JTPA at $980 million in FY 1989 and "such sums as necessary" for subsequent years. The generic program operates on a program year, rather than on a fiscal year basis, with program years running from July 1 to June 30. In other words, appropriations for FY1993 are spent during program year 1993, which begins July 1, 1993, and ends June 30, 1994.

Clean Air Employment Transition Assistance. CAETA was added to title III of JTPA by the Clean Air Act Amendments of 1990 ad is authorized at $50 million for FY1991 and such sums as may be necessary for FY1992 through FY 1995. The total appropriation for the 5 fiscal years cannot exceed $250 million. Like the generic program, CAETA operates on a program year beginning July 1.

Defense Conversion Assistance. DCA was added to title III of JTPA by the National Defense Authorization Act for FY1991 and is authorized at $150 million for FY1991. While under the authorization act the funds wee to be available until expended, the Defense Appropriations Act for FY1991 provided that the funds were available only through September 30,1 993. The Dire Emergency Supplemental Appropriations Act, 1992 (P.L. 102-368) extended the availability of funds to September 30, 1997.

Defense Diversification. The Defense Diversification program was added to title III of JTPA by the National Defense Authorization Act for FY 1993 and is authorized at $75 million for FY 1993.

APPROPRIATIONS

Table 1. Appropriations History of Title III Programs
(in millions of $)

FY	Generic program	CAETA	DCA	Defense divers
1983	$110.0	--	--	--
TP[a]	94.0	--	--	--
1984	223.3	--	--	--
1985	222.5	--	--	--
1986	95.6	--	--	--
1987	200.0	--	--	--
1988	287.2	--	--	--
1989	283.8	--	--	--
1990	463.6	--	--	--
1991	527.0	--	$150.0[b]	--
1992	527.0	$50.0[c]	--	--
1993	516.6	50.0	--	$75.0[d]

[a] The transition period (TP) was the 9-month period form Oct. 1, 1993, thorugh June 30, 1994. After this period, JTPA operated on a "forward funded" program year of July 1 through June 30, rather than on a fiscal year of Oct. 1 through Sept. 30.

[b] These funds, appropriated by the Defense Appropriations Act for FY 1991 (P.L. 101-511), were transferred from the Department of Defense to the Department of Labor for the Defense Conversion Adjustment (DCA) grant progra, and are available form July 1, 1991, through Sept. 30, 1997.

[c] These funds are available Oct. 1, 1991, through June 30, 1993.

[d] Of funds appropriated by the Naitonal Defense Appropriations aCt, 1993, it appears that the Secretary of Defense may expend $75 million to fund a new JTPA Defense Diversificaiton program authorized by the National Defense Authorizatin Act for 1993.

ALLOCATION OF FUNDS

Generic program. Of the funds appropriated for the generic program, 80 percent is for a "formula" grant program and 20 percent is reserved for national activities including a discretionary grant program. AT least 10 percent of the funds reserved by the Secretary of Labor for national activities is to be used to fund demonstration projects.

Discretionary grants are available for a variety of dislocate worker projects including those that provide services needed as a result of mass layoffs, which may be caused by, among other factors, natural disasters of Federal Government actions. States may apply for the grants, but in accordance with DOL application procedures they must indicate why a proposed project cannot be funded with the funds allocated through the "formula" grant program.

In the "formula" grant program, funds are allocated to States on the basis of a three part formula: one-third based on relative number of unemployed, one-third based on relative number of unemployed individuals in excess of 4.5 percent of the labor force, ad one-third based on relative number of individuals unemployed 15 weeks or longer.[5] Governors may reserve up to 40 percent of this State allocation for State level activities. Another 10 percent can be reserved for distribution during the first 9 months of the program year to local areas with unforeseen need. AT least 50 percent of a State's allocation must be passed through to substate areas by a State formula. To receive funds, States must submit a plan every 2 years to the Secretary of Labor describing the programs and activities that will be provided, and must have an identifiable State dislocated worker unit capable of responding quickly in cases of layoffs or plant closings to assess needs and provide basic services.

To receive funds at the local level, a substate grantee must submit a plan for approval by the Governor detailing how services will be provided within the substate area. Substate areas are designated by the Governor. A substate grantee is designated through an agreement among the Governor, the local elected officials and the Private Industry Councils (PICs) in the area.[6] A substate grantee may be a PIC, an existing grantee or administrative entity under JTPA, a private nonprofit organization, a local government agency, the local office of a State agency, or another public agency such as a community college or area vocational school.

Defense Conversion Assistance. DCA funds are available through DOL. States, substate grantees, employers, employer associations, and representatives of employees may apply for these grants to serve workers dislocated as a result of cuts in defense of base closures. Under the DCA program, the Secretary of Labor is also authorized to make grant awards to fund demonstration projects to encourage and promote innovative responses to dislocation which results from cuts in defense spending and from base closings. In

---

[5] The Secretary of Labor is requred to collect data on plant closings and permanent layoffs and on dislocated farmers and ranchers. Once th e data onplant colsong and permanent layoffs are abvialble, 75 percent of title II State allotments will be based on thethree factors described above, and the remaiing 25 percent will be based on each State's share of total dislcoated workers, ans determined by the data on plant closing and mass ayoffs and when available, by the data on dislocated farmers and ranchers.

[6] Each substate area must have a PIC which provides policy guidance on JTPA activities conductd in the substate area dn oversees the local job training programs. A majority of the members must be representatives of the private sector. Other members include representatives of organized labor, community-based organizations, educational agencies, vocational rehabilitation agencies, public assistance agencies, economic developmetn agencies and the public employment service.

November, 1992, the Secretary of Labor announced the award of about $5 million dollars for 12 demonstration projects.

Clean Air Employment Transition Assistance. CAETA funds are available through DOL. States, substate grantees, employers, employer association, and representatives of employees may apply for these grants to serve workers dislocated as a result of compliance with the Clean Air Act.

Defense Diversification. Like the DCA and CAETA programs, funds will be available through a grant application process. Eligible applicants will include States, substate grantees, employers, representatives of employees, labor-management committees, and other employer-employee entities. Also, under the Defense Diversification program the Secretary of Defense can reserve 10 percent of the funds appropriated for demonstration projects.

ELIGIBLE WORKERS

Generic program. Persons eligible for services:

- individuals who have lost their job or received notice of termination, who are eligible for unemployment compensation or who have exhausted their unemployment compensation, and who are unlikely to return to their previous industry or occupation;

- persons who have been terminated or received a notice of termination as a result of a permanent closing or substantial layoff at a plant, facility or enterprise;[7]

- long-term unemployed individuals with limited opportunities for employment or reemployment in the same or similar occupation in the are in which the individual resides, including older workers whose age creates a barrier to employment, and

- self-employed individuals, including farmers and ranchers, who are unemployed as a result of general economic conditions or natural disasters.[8]

Most dislocated workers can begin receiving most basic readjustment services (see **Types of Assistance**, below) when a public announcement that a facility is closing is made an can receive all services 180 days before the facility is scheduled to close even if the worker has not received a specific notice of termination or lay off. Table 2 shows the characteristics of participants in the generic program for Program Year 1990.

Defense Conversion Assistance. Persons eligible for services under the DCA program must meet the eligibility criteria for the eugenic program and have been laid off or terminated or received a notice of layoff or termination as a result of reductions in defense spending or base closures. As in the generic program, workers eligible for DCA can begin receiving most based readjustment services when a public announcement that a facility is scheduled to close even if the worker has not received a specific notice of termination or lay off. In addition, civilian employees of the Department of Defense (DOD)

---

[7] Regulations define substantial layoff as a layoff afffecting at least one-third of the employees if the one-third is equal to at least 50 employees, or at least 500 employees.

[8] In addition, displaced homemakers may receive servies if the Governor determines tha tthey can be served without adversely affecting services to toher dislocated workers.

can receive services up to 2 years before a military installation is closed or the realignment of the installation is completed.

Table 2. Participants in Title III, JTPA, July 1990-June 1992

Total Number	107,500
Male	57%
Female	43%
White	75%
Black	14%
Hispanic	9%
Other	3%
19-21	3%
22-54 years old	88%
55 and older	9%
economically disadvantaged	28%
Unemployment compensation claimant	55%
Public assistance recipient	7%
School dropout	14%
Student	1%
High school graduate (or More)	85%

Source: U.S. Department of Labor. Job Training Quarterly Survey. JTPA Title IIA and III Enrollment and Termination During Program Year 1990 (July 1990-June 1991.) Washington, Jan. 1992. Table 25.

Clean Air Employment Transition Assistance. Persons eligible for services under the CAETA program must meet the eligibility criteria for the generic program and have been laid off or terminated or received a notice of layoff or termination as a result of compliance with the Clean Air Act. As in the generic program, workers eligible for CAETA can begin receiving most basic readjustment services when a public announcement that a facility is closing is made a can receive all services 180 days before the facility is scheduled to close even if the worker has not received a specific notice of termination or lay off.

Defense Diversification. Persons eligible for services are:

- Members of the armed services who were on active duty or full-time National Guard duty on September 30, 1990, and who during the next 5 years are involuntarily separated from duty or separated as part of a special separation benefits program or a DOD voluntary separation incentive program if they are not entitled to retired or retainer pay and apply for the program's services within 180 days of separation from duty.

- Civilian employees of the DOD the Department of Energy who were terminated or laid off or received a notice of termination of layoff as a result of reductions in defense spending during the 5-year period beginning October 1, 1992, if they are not entitled to retired or retainer pay. IN the case of a notice of termination or layoff, employees shall not be eligible for services until 180 days before the projected date of termination of layoff. Civilian DOD employees working at a military installation being closed or realigned can receive services up to 2 years before military installation is closed or the realignment of the installation is completed.

- Defense contractor employees who are terminated or laid off or received a notice of termination or layoff as a result of reductions in defense spending or the closure or realignment of a military installation during ht e5-year period beginning October 1, 1992, if they are not entitled to retired or retainer pay. (The defense contractor must have one or more contracts with DOD totaling at least $550,000 or have one or more subcontracts in connection with a defense contract totaling at least $500,000.)

TYPES OF ASSISTANCE

RAPID RESPONSE

Generic program. These services are provided through specialists in the State dislocated worker unit, who make immediate contact (preferably within 48 hours) with employer and employee organizations after learning of a current or projected facility closure or a substantial layoff.[9] In addition to providing information about existing programs and emergency assistance when necessary, rapid response teams attempt to establish labor-management committees to develop strategies to deal with the employment and training needs of affected workers.[10] Rapid response services also include gathering information on economic dislocations and resources for displaced workers within the State, working with economic development agencies to prevent layoffs and and dislocations, information dissemination on the services of the services of the dislocated workers unit, and assistance to local communities in developing a response to dislocations and in gaining access to State economic development assistance. States use their "40 percent" funds reserved for State activities to provide rapid response services.

Defense conversion assistance. Same as the generic program.

Clean Air Employment Transition Assistance. Same as the generic program.

Defense Diversification. Same as the generic program except that under the Defense Diversification program, the grant applicant must provide verification that the State dislocated worker unit is providing rapid response services. The Secretary of Denfense is required to withhold 25 percent of the grant award until the Secretary has determined that the applicant is satisfactorily implementing the activies described in the grant application. Up to 20 percent of the amount retained, not exceed $50,000, is to be used to reimburse the State dislocated worker for expenses incurred in providing rapid response and other early intervention services if these have been adequately.

---

[9] For the purpose of proiding rapid response, substantial layoff means a lyoff of 50 or more individuals.

[10] Labor-managemtn committees are defined in the law as voluntary committes ttypically characterized by the following: shared and equal particpation by workers and managemetn; shared financial particpatin between the company and the State for the committee's operating expenses; a chairpaerson jointly selected by labor and managmenet who is not employed by either labor or management and who provides advice and leadership to the committee; capabole of responding flexibly to worker needs; operating under a formal agreement; and proviving local job identification activities on behalf of affected workers.

BASIC READJUSTMENT

Generic program. These services may include development of individual readjustment plans, outreach and intake, early readjustment assistance, job or career counseling, testing, orientations, assessment, determination of occupational skills, provision of "world-of-work" and occupational information, job placement assistance, labor market information, job clubs, job search, job development, supportive services (including child care and transportation allowances), pre-layoff assistance, relocation assistance, and early intervention programs conducted in cooperation with employers or labor organizations in the event of a facility closing.

Workers can begin receiving all of these services except for supportive services and relocation assistance when a public announcement that a facility is closing is made even if the worker has not received a specific notice of termination or lay off. When basic readjustment services are provided to these workers who have not yet received specific notices, the services are to be provided (to the extent practicable) with the State's "40 percent" funds reserved for State activities.

Defense Conversion Assistance. Same as the generic program.

Clean Air Employment Transition Assistance. Same as the generic program.

Defense Diversification. Same as the generic program.

RETRAINING

Generic program. Retraining services may include classroom training, occupational skill training, on-job-training, out-of-area job search, relocation, basic and remedial education, literacy training and English-as-a-second-language, entrepreneurial training, and other appropriate activities related to actual job opportunities in the local area.

At least 50 percent of funds in a substate area must be used for retraining services. In certain cases, a local area may receive a waiver from this requirement, but in no case may less than 30 percent of funds in a substate area be spent for retraining services.

Also, a substate grantee, if appropriate, may issue a "certificate of continuing eligibility": to a dislocated workers, rather than provide services immediately after the worker applies for assistance. The worker remains eligible for services for up to 104 weeks, and may use the certificate to arrange his own retraining services, subject to the approval of the substate grantee and the availability of funds.

Defense Conversion Assistance. The retraining services that may be provided are the same as under the generic program.

Clean Air Employment Transition Assistance. Same as DCA, except that under CAETA the Act establishes specific requirements for expenditures for job search and relocation allowances. Job search and relocation outside the commuting area in which the worker lives are permitted only when no suitable employment is available within commuting distance. The cost allowed for job search may not exceed 90 percent of an individual's expenses and may not exceed a total of $800. The cost of relocation may not exceed 90 percent of the expenses and may not exceed a total of $800 without justification in the grant application and the approval of the DOL grant officer.

Defense Diversification. Same as CAETA.

NEEDS-RELATED PAYMENTS

Generic program. Person eligible for cash assistance, referred to as needs-related payments, are those workers who are unemployed and do not qualify for unemployment compensation (UC), or have exhausted their benefits, ad need income support to participate in education or training.

To receive payments, workers must have enrolled in training by the end of the 13th week of receiving unemployment compensation benefits, or by the end of the 8th week after being informed that short-term layoff will actually exceed 6 months.

No more than 25 percent of funds expended by the local area may be used for needs-related payments and other supportive services, such as child care, and transportation assistance.

Defense Conversion Assistance. Same as the generic program, except the statute does not have a cost limitation on needs-related payments and other supportive services.

Clean Air Employment Transition Assistance. Persons eligible for needs-related payments are those dislocated workers who do not qualify for unemployment compensation (UC), or have exhausted their benefits, and need income support to participate in education or training and whose total family income does not exceed the lower living standard income level.[11] Under CAETA needs-related payments may not exceed the higher of an individual's UC benefit or the poverty level as defined by the Office of Management and Budget.[12] AS in the generic program, to receive payments, workers must have enrolled in training by the end of the 13th week of receiving unemployment compensation benefits, or by the end of the 8th weeks after being informed that short-term layoff will actually exceed 6 months. Also under CAETA, a grant application must contain assurances that grant funds will be used to provide needs-related payments.

Defense Diversification. As in CAETA, persons eligible for needs-related payments are those dislocated workers who do not qualify for unemployment compensation (UC), or have exhausted their benefits, and need income support to participate in education or training and whose total family income does not exceed the lower living standard income level. Under the Defense Diversification program, priority for needs related payments is to be given to individuals participating in certificate or degree awarding vocational training or education programs. As in CAETA, needs-related payments may not exceed the higher of an individual's UC benefit or the poverty level as defined by the Office of Management and Budget. As in the generic program, to receive payments, workers must have also enrolled in training by the end of the 13th week of receiving unemployment compensation benefits, or by the end of the 8th weeks after being informed that short-term layoff will actually exceed 6 months.

OTHER SERVICES

Defense Diversification. In addition to providing rapid response services, basic readjustment services, retraining, and income support, funds may also be used to : (1) provide skills upgrading for non-managerial employees to replace or update obsolete skills

---

[11] The lower living standard inocme level (LLSIL) is established for metropolitan and non-metropolitan regions of the country, for Alaska, Hawaii, and Guam, and for 25 selected Metrolpolitan Statistical Areas. By region, the most recent LLSIL figures published by the Department of Labor (April 3, 1992) range form $!9,800 for a family of 4 in the non-metropolitan South to $14,160 for a family of 4 in the metropolitan Northeast.

[12] For 1992, the poverty income guideline is $13,950 for a familhy of 4 except in Alaska and Hawaii where it is higher.

and (2) to promote the development of high performance workplace systems, employee and participative management systems, and workforce participation in the evaluation, selection, and implementation of new production technologies.

CREATING A FEDERAL EMPLOYMENT AND TRAINING SYSTEM: AN OVERVIEW

Richard N. Apling and Ann Lordeman

SUMMARY

The Administration and many Members of Congress maintain that improving the skills of current and future workers will promote U.S. economic growth and prosperity. Recently, for example, Secretary of Labor Robert B. Reich wrote that "up-to-date skills become ever more crucial - even in jobs where the unskilled could formerly thrive. Workers without skills, meanwhile, find their options shrinking."[1] AT the same time, many observers have become increasingly concerned that we have no Federal Training system but rather piecemeal approaches represented by the large number of Federal employment and training programs spread across numerous Federal agencies. This report examines these concerns and some of the proposed approaches for creating a more coherent Federal system:

- Eliminating programs,
- Consolidating programs, and
- Coordinating programs

FEDERAL PROGRAMS

The General Accounting Office (GAO) estimates[2] that $24 billion in FY 1993 was spread among more than 150 Federal employment and training programs[3] in 14 agencies. No

---

[1] Reich, Robert B. Jobs: Skills Before Credetnials. Wall Street Journal, Feb. 2, 19945. p. A18.

[2] GAO data reported here come from a table presented in testimony before the Senate Appropriations Subcommittee on Labor, Health and Human Services, and Educatio in June 1993.

[3] There is some disagreement about which Federal programs should be cunted as employmetn and training funding. For example, the GAO includes Departmtn of Eduation adult literacy programs sucha s Literacy for Incarcerated Adults. While literacy level is no doubt related to the ability to obtain ad hold a job, some observers have a norrower definition of employemtn and training and would not count such programs. The GAO aslo lists student fiancnial aid programs sucha as Pell Grants and Federal Family Education Loans. Since these programs hielp studnets finance a wide variety of postsecondary education, some argue that they should not be counted as job training programs. Others maintain that a large protion of these funds that finance student attendance at less-than-4-year institutions should be counted as Federal training funding.

one questions that there are numerous training and training-related programs. AT the same time, it is important to realize that most of these programs are quite small and narrowly focused: Many programs GAO lists receive less than $10 million, some have never been funded, and many have relatively narrow purposes or target particular populations such as displaced homemakers, single parents, or Native Hawaiians. On the other hand, a few large programs provide most of the Federal resources for training. Specifically 11 programs in the Departments of Education, Labor, ad Health and Human Services account for about 75 percent of the employment and training funds GAO identities.[4] (See the table at the end of the report.)

ELIMINATE PROGRAMS

One approach to building a Federal training system from this complex array of large a dismal Federal programs would be to eliminate some of them. A possible strategy would be to examine the effectiveness of all training programs, continue to fund those that work, and eliminate those that are ineffective or have accomplished their goals. One case in which the Administration is pursuing this approach is the FY1995 budget request to increase funding for the Job Training Partnership act (JTPA) Adult Training Program (title II A) and cut the Youth Training Program (title II C) because of evaluation results. While it seems logical to eliminate programs that do not work or are no longer needed, this is not always straight forward. Often it is difficult to reach consensus on which programs are and are not working and, even if there were evidence that a program could be eliminated, eliminating even small programs can be politically difficult. For example, the last several Administrations have recommended eliminating the consumer and Home-making Education program which is part of the Carl D. Perkins Vocational and Applied Technology Education Act. In 1993 the Acting Assistant Secretary for Vocational and Adult Education testified that "all States currently have active, well-established consumer and homemaking programs that will continue without direct Federal support. States and localities can also, if they choose, use funds from their [basic Perkins grant] to support consumer an homemaking education."[5] Despite annual recommendations to eliminate this $35 million program advocates for Consumer and Homemaking education have successfully persuaded both the relevant authorizing and appropriating committees to continue it. The Administration has again recommended eliminating Consumer and Homemaking Education for FY 1995.

CONSOLIDATE PROGRAMS

A second approach would be to consolidate programs. Under this approach, the resources of categorical programs are combined, and local entities or States are given discretion in deciding how funds should be spent to achieve the objectives of the authorizing legislation. Currently, the Administration is proposing to consolidate six Depart-

---

[4] Including All-Volunteer Force Educational Assistance (Montgomery GI Bill) in the Department of Veterans Affairs would account for about 78 percnet of these funds. We have omitted thsi program form our table becasue veterans' programs are not usually included in proposals to create a coordinated training system.

[5] U.S. Congress. House. Appropriations Committee. Labor, Health and Human Services, Education, ad Related Agencies Subcommittee. Departmtn of Labor, Health ad Human Services, Education, and Related Agencies Appropriations for 1994. Hearing, 103d Cong., 1st Sess., May 7, 1993. Washington GPO, 1993. p. 369.

ment of Labor programs for dislocated workers into one comprehensive program.[6] Problems sometime arise when programs are consolidated. For example, it becomes more difficult to ensure that particular populations are served and to account for how funds re specifically spent. As a result, categorical programs may be added to the legislation. For example, program consolidation was the original approach of JTPA. Categorical programs were later added to the statute: 7 programs were authorized in 1982; in 1992, 15 were authorized. (For FY 1994, Congress appropriated funds for 10 of these programs.)

COORDINATE PROGRAMS

A third approach would be to coordinate programs.[7] One strategy to promote program coordination is to authorize waivers of statutory and regulatory requirements that some argue prevent or hinder program coordination. A second strategy is to change program requirements, definitions, etc., so that they are the same form program to program. This has been done, for example, with the definition of "displaced homemaker" in JTPA and in the Displaced Homemaker Self-Sufficiency Act. Program advocates and advocates for special populations such s the disabled warn that waivers that other program coordination strategies can impede program accountability and reduce program access for target groups. In response to these concerns, coordination provisions are often limited. For example, waiver authorities may not extend to central program purposes and provisions such as targeting provisions. Ironically, some argue, the provisions that are preserved are the most likely to hinder coordination.

A third coordination strategy would be to retain categorical programs, but create single points of entries in communities to several different federally funded employment and training programs. These points of entry are commonly referred to as "one-stop" centers. Under this approach, an individual would not go to several places to learn about he array of programs and services available, but would obtain information about them in "one-stop". The centers could facilitate coordination if there was a common intake procedure administered by the center or the center could serve only as a referral source to other programs. The Administration has announced that it intends to propose legislation to foster "one-stop" career enters. Republican members of the House Education and Labor Committee have also proposed to foster one-stop centers, called community job resource centers (H.R. 2943). This approach has the advantage or ensuring that programs designed to serve specific populations are retained, but like the other approaches it also faces political considerations, e.g., which entities should serve as the centers (e.g., the Employment Service, community colleges, Private Industry Councils) and how should these entities be chosen? In addition, simply creating "one-stop" centers would help provide information about various training programs but would not ensure that these programs are coordinated.

---

[6] These programs are trade Adjustmetn Assistnace, North American Free Trade Agreement (NAFTA) Transistional Adjustment Assitance Program, Economic Dislocation and Worker Adjsutment Assistance (EDWAA), Defense Conversion Adjustment, Clean Air Employment Transiton Assistance, and the Defense Diversification Program. See: Department of Labor. FY 1995 budget Justificiatons. p. TES-46.

[7] For additional information on cocordianted services, see: U.S. Library of Congress. Congressional Research Service. Linking Human Services: An Overview of Coordination and Integreton Efforts. CRS Report for Congress No. 93-369 EPW, by Ruth Ellen Wasem. Washington, Mar. 30, 1993.

Major Federally Funded Employment and Training Programs[a]
(dollars in millions)

Program	Purpose	Funding mechanisms	FY 1994 appropriation	FY 1995 request
Department of Labor				
JTPA Adult Training Program	To prepare low-income adults (age 22 and older) for jobs by providing training, remedial education, and related services	Formula grants to States and local entities	$ 988	$1,130
JTPA Summer Youth Employment and Training Programs	To enhance the basic educational skills of low-income youth (age 14-21) and expose them to the world of work by providing jobs, remedial education, and academic enrichment	Formula grants to States and local entities	888	1,056
JTPA Youth Training Program	To improve the long-term employability of low-income youth (age 14-21) by providing training, education, and related services	Formula grants to States and local entities	658	599
JTPA Dislocated Worker Program (EDWAA)	To assist workers who lose their jobs and are unlikely to return to them to become re-employed by providing early intervention services, retraining, and cash assistance based on need	Formula grants to States and local entities	1,118	1,465
JTPA Job Corps	To assist youth (age 14-24), who both need and can benefit from intensive services provided primarily in a residential setting "to become more responsible, employable, and productive citizens"	Federally administered primarily through contracts with corporations and nonprofit organization	1,040	1,157

Major Federally Funded Employment and Training Programs[a]--Continued
(dollars in millions)

Program	Purpose	Funding mechanisms	FY 1994 appropriation	FY 1995 request
U. S. Employment Services (Wagner Peyser Act)--State allotments	To serve as a public labor exchange for individuals seeking jobs and for employers seeking workers	Formula grants to States	$ 833	$ 847
Department of Health and Human Services				
Job Opportunities and Basic Skills (JOBS) program	To enable recipients of Aid to Families with Dependent Children (AFDC) to obtain the education, training, and employment that will avoid long-term welfare dependence	Formula grants to States	1,100	1,300
Department of Education				
Vocational Rehabilitation Program--State grants	To provide comprehensive vocational rehabilitation services to help individuals with physical and mental disabilities become employable and to achieve economic self-sufficiency, independence, and inclusion and integration with society	Formula grants to States	1,968	2,021
Carl D. Perkins Vocational and Applied Technology Education Act-- basic State grants	To improve the quality of vocational education "with the full participation" of students who are members of "special populations," which include the disabled, the economical and educationally disadvantaged, and the limited-English proficient	Formula grants to States	962	963

Major Federally Funded Employment and Training Programs[a]--Continued
(dollars in millions)

Program	Purpose	Funding mechanisms	FY 1994 appropriation	FY 1995 request
Federal Family Education Loans (FFEL)[b]	To provide federally guaranteed loans to support the cost of attendance at postsecondary institutions including colleges, universities, community colleges, technical institutes, and trade schools	Privately capitalized federally guaranteed loans	not available[c]	not available[c]
Pell Grants[b]	To provide "foundation" grants to undergraduates to help pay for education after high school	Federal grants to eligible students	$2,383	$2,417

[a]All-Volunteer Force Educational Assistance in the Department of Veterans Affairs (Montgomery GI Bill) is not included because veterans' programs are not usually incorporated in proposals to create a coordinated training system.

[b]The FFEL and Pell programs help finance students' postsecondary education and thus are not job training programs. However, both programs provide funding to students undertaking postsecondary occupational training at community colleges and proprietary schools. Funding reported here reflects estimates that 21 percent of Pell grants (in FY 1991) and 15.4 percent of FFEL loans (in FY 1992) went to students attending proprietary schools. Since an estimated 70 percent of community college students pursue occupational training, we have included funding for 70 percent of the proportions of these programs received by community college students (i.e., 70 percent of 6 percent of the FFEL volume and 70 percent of 24 percent of Pell grants).

[c]Federal funding for the FFEL program includes multi-year costs for loan subsidies and default reimbursements. It is not possible to allocate these costs to students attending postsecondary occupational training programs. One indication of the overall size of this investment is the loan volume (or loan amounts disbursed) for proprietary school students and vocational students in community colleges. For FY 1994, total loan volume is estimated at $18.2 billion. Of this amount, about $3.6 billion would be received by proprietary school students (based on 15.4 percent of total volume in FY 1992) and vocational students at community colleges (70 percent of 6.1 percent of the total volume in FY 1992).

THE PROPOSED REEMPLOYMENT ACT OF 1994: A FACT SHEET

James R. Storey and Ann M. Lordeman
Education and Public Welfare Division

INTRODUCTION

The Reemployment Act of 1994 (H.R. 4040/S. 1951), submitted to Congress by President Clinton on March 16, 1994, is intended to expand and improve Government efforts to help workers find new careers after permanent job loss. The bill, which would replace six existing dislocated worker programs, would offer a wide range of employment services to dislocated workers. Services would be provided either through career centers serving only dislocated workers or though voluntary "one-stop career centers" for the general public. Clients with a job tenure of at least 1 year with the former employer would receive "retraining income support" in the form of extended weekly unemployment compensation (UC). Most features of this new program would take effect on July 1, 1995, under the administration of the U.S. Department of Labor (DOL). The Administration estimates the bill would increase current-law costs by $13 billion during the 5-year period from FY 1995 through FY 1999. Outlays from the Unemployment Trust Fund would account for $2 billion of this amount. The $!3 billion increase over 5 years would be in addition to a $1.5 billion increase requested for dislocated worker assistance in the President's FY 1995 budget.

COMPREHENSIVE PROGRAM FOR WORKER REEMPLOYMENT

Six programs now provide assistance to dislocated workers: Trade Adjustment Assistance, North American Free Trade Agreement Transitional Adjustment Assistance, Economic Dislocation and Worker Adjustment Assistance (EDWAA), Defense Conversion Adjustment, Clean Air Employment Transition Assistance, and the Defense Diversification Program. Except for EDWAA, each program aids only workers who have permanently lost their jobs as a result of a specific Federal policy.

Under the proposal, all permanently laid-off workers, regardless of the cause of dislocation, could receive: "basic reemployment" services, such as assistance in filing an initial UC claim. preliminary assessment of skill levels ad service needs; job search assistance, including resume and interview preparation; and job referral and job placement assistance. Workers who do not obtain jobs through these services would be eligible for : "intensive reemployment" services, such as diagnostic testing and the development of an individual reemployment plan; education and training serves, including basic skills and occupational skills training; and retraining income support. In addition, supportive serves, such as transportation and dependent care, would be made available to dislocated workers when needed to participate in intensive reemployment services and in education and training and could be made available when needed to participate in basic reemployment services. Generally, funds for services would be allocated to States and localities by dol using a formula based on unemployment measures.

Retraining Income Support

To be eligible for retaining income support, a claimant would have to begin an approved training course by the later of the 16th week of UC eligibility or the 14th week after finding that the claimant's layoff was permanent. A 30-day delay could be authorized under certain circumstances. Income support would be contingent on satisfactory progress in retraining.

Claimants whose job tenure with the layoff employer was at lest 3 years would be eligible for up to 52 weeks of benefits; those with tenures of at lest 1 year but less than 3 years could receive up to 26 weeks of benefits. The benefit amount would equal the State UC benefit ad be paid after all regular and extended UC benefits were exhausted. Claimants age 55 or older could receive instead a wage subsidy if the only work they could find paid less than 80 percent of their previous wage.

Benefits would be paid from the Unemployment Trust Fund, funded by a 0.2 percent tax on the first $7,000 of annual wages of each worker covered by UC. However, benefits for workers with job tenures less than 3 years would be paid from general funds until July 1, 1999. Wage subsidies would be paid from general funds indefinitely.

Career Centers

Access to employment services would be through either mandated career centers or voluntary "one-stop" career centers. Career centers would provide only dislocated workers with access to information and services, while one-stop career centers would have to serve dislocated workers but could also serve other individuals and employers.

Centers could be operated either by individual entities or consortia, including the Employment Service, the substate grantee of the new program, a unit of government, community colleges, and community-based organizations. Career centers could be established by the substate grantee responsible for operating the new program. One-stop career centers would be "charted" by Workforce Investment Boards consisting of representatives from private employers, organized labor, community-based organizations, educational institutions, community leaders, and local elected officials.

Other Provisions

The bill would allow States the option under UC to pay reemployment bonuses for selected UC claimants who found new work within a specified time period, ad to pay partial UC benefits if an employer elected to reduce the work hours for a large group of workers rather than lay off a smaller number of workers. The bill would establish a national labor market information system. To promote program innovation (named "Reinvention Labs"), it also would amend the Job Training Partnership Act to allow waivers of requirements governing programs for the economically disadvantaged.

JOB OPPORTUNITIES AND BASIC SKILLS (JOBS) PROGRAM: BASIC FACTS

Vee Burke

The Job Opportunities and Basic Skills (JOBS) program, which took effect nationwide in FY 1991, has changed the thrust and scope of Federal efforts dating back to 1967 to promote employability of welfare mothers. Unlike the predecessor work incentive (WIN) work/training program for families enrolled in the program of Aid to Families with Dependent Children (AFDC), JOBS requires participation of most mothers with children as young as 3 (WIN excused mothers with preschoolers), stresses education, and explicitly allows postsecondary education. Further, it offers States much more Federal money than WIN did.

> Title IV, Part F, the Social Security Act, JOBS:
>
> *"IT is the purpose of this part to assure that needy families with children obtain the education, training, and employment that will help them avoid long-term welfare dependence."*

Data from the Department of Health and Human Services (DHHS) indicate that JOBS is stressing development of human capital (education and job skills). Forty percent of FY 1992 participants engaged in an educational activity, about 21 percent in vocational training, job skills, or job readiness, and 9 percent in job search. In contrast, only 5.5. percent of participants in the pre-JOBS WIN demonstration program in FY 1985 were engaged in education and 2.3 percent in vocational skills, but 52 percent in job search (General Accounting Office Report HRD 87-34). Congress appropriated $1 billion yearly for JOBS in FY 1991-93, compared to $127 million for WIN in FY 1987, but States, which must match Federal dollars, spent only abut $1.9 billion of the available $3 billion. State funds accounted for about 39 percent of total FY 1993 JOBS expenditures. During FY 1991-92, the average monthly number of AFDC adults engaged in JOBS activities has been almost 500,000. However, many of these persons did not meet the definition of JOBS "participant" used to determine a State's participation rate. The U.S. participation rate in FY 1992 was 16 percent, above the then required rte of 11 percent. State rates varied; the rate was below 10 percent in Indiana and Maine, but about 25 percent in Alabama, Idaho, Massachusetts, Nebraska (77 percent), New Mexico, North Dakota, Oklahoma, Utah, the Virgin Islands, Washington, Wisconsin, and Wyoming.

BASIC PROVISIONS OF JOBS: DESCRIPTION AND DATA

[Note: Data below relate to average monthly national numbers; State numbers vary widely. Also, the description of "required" JOBS provisions needs qualification; they are required only to the extent that State resources otherwise permit.]

Who Must Participate? Generally, AFDC parents whose youngest child is at lest 3 and high school dropout parents with younger children. In FY 1994, each State must engage in JOBS 15 percent of all "non-exempt" AFDC adult recipients, but a much higher percentage of adults in AFDC-UP (unemployed-parent) families. Beginning in FY 1994, one parent in 40 percent of these two-parent families must spend at least 16 hours weekly in a work program. States failing participation standards receive lower Federal matching rates.

What Educational Services Must Be Offered? To Whom? High school or equivalent education, basic ad remedial education, and education for persons with limited English proficiency. Most young AFDC mothers (those under 20) who failed to complete high school must be required to participate din an :educational activity" even if they have an infant; this is sometimes called learnfare for parents. In addition, States may enroll AFDC recipients in postsecondary education in "appropriate cases." IN FY 1992, 25.1 percent of participants were engaged in high school or equivalent education (including basic adult education and English as a second language), and 15.1 percent in postsecondary education , including 6.9 percent in self-initiated schooling beyond high school.

What Job Services Must Be Offered? Job skills training, job readiness activities, and job development and placement.

What Other Serves Must Be Offered? Two of these four: community work experience,(SWEP) (workfare, with hours based on the AFDC grant) or an alternative work experience program (full-time work may be required), work supplementation (a person's AFDC grant subsidizes a job), on-the-job training, and job search. In FY 1992, 3.6 percent of participants were in CEWP; fewer than 0.5 percent each were in work supplementation or on-the-job-training. Nineteen jurisdictions reported no se of CWEP.

What Support Services are Required? Child care must be "guaranteed" for children under 13 (otherwise, the mother's participation cannot be required) and necessary work expenses reimbursed. States must provide transitional benefits to families who work their way off AFDC: subsidized day care benefits for 1 year and Medicaid for 6 months plus an offer of another 6 months of medial aid to those whose family income, net of child care costs, is below 185 percent of the poverty guideline. In the fourth quarter of FY 1991, a monthly average of 147,415 families (218,003 children) received AFDC-related child care; one-eighth of the families were ex-AFDC families. Outlays for AFDC-related child care totaled $755 million in FY 1992 (about $165 million for transitional care).

How is JOBS Funded? The law "entitles" each State to a share of JOBS funds equal to its share of adult AFDC recipients. However, only 17 States spent enough in FY 1993 to qualify for their full share. The Federal "enhanced" matching rate for JOBS activities and costs of full-time personnel generally ranges form 60-80 percent , with rates inversely related to per capita income; States failing participation standards and/or target group spending ratios receive only 50 percent. For administrative expenses other than full-time personnel and for work-related expenses other than child care) separately funded), the JOBS matching rate is 50 percent.

How Are Funds Targeted? To receive the enhanced Federal matching rate, States must use at lest 55 percent of JOBS funds on target groups: custodial parents under age 24 without a high school diploma or recent work history, parents enrolled for 36 months (groups considered likely to become long-term AFDC users), and parents whose youngest child is at lest 16 years old)and, hence, within 2 years of losing eligibility).

Issue: Should Congress Expand JOBS Funding? Since JOBS got underway, record-breaking AFDC caseloads and sharp increases in Medicaid have strained State budgets, led to some benefit cuts, and produced a difficult environment. The 102d Congress voted to offer States an extra $100 million each for FY 1993 and FY 1994 and to reduce the State matching share of JOBS costs for 3 years, but these provisions died with the pocket veto of the Revenue Act of 1992. (S. 16, introduced January 21, 1993, would provide "full" funding for JOBS (100 percent Federal funding for new sums.)

THE JOB TRAINING PARTNERSHIP ACT:
TRAINING PROGRAMS AT A GLANCE

Molly Forman and Ann Lordeman

The Job Training Partnership Act (JTPA), first enacted din 1982, is the country's chief training legislation. JTPA is primarily composed of program focusing on the training needs of economically disadvantaged individuals facing significant barriers to employment. Programs are administered by the Department of Labor. FY 1994 appropriation for JTPA programs total $5.0 billion. Unless otherwise noted, FY 1994 appropriations are for JTPA program year 1994 (July 1, 1994 through June 30, 1995).

Adult training program (title II-A)
Eligibility: age 22 and older, at least 90 percent economically disadvantaged, at least 65 percent "hard to serve"; *Administration*: formula grants to State and local entities; *FY 1994 Appropriation*: $988.0 million

Summer youth training program (title II-B)
Eligibility: age 14-21, economically disadvantaged; Administration: formula grants to State and local entities; *FY 1994 Appropriation*: $888.3 million. Of this amount, $682.3 million was appropriated for the summer of 1995. The remainder supplements the $670.7 million appropriated I FY 1993 for the summer of 1994.

Youth Training program (title II-C)
Eligibility: age 14-21, at lest 90 percent economically disadvantaged, at lest 65 percent "hard to serve", at least 50 percent out of school; *Administration*: formula grants to State and local entities; *FY 1994 Appropriation*: $658.7 million.

"Generic" program for dislocated workers (title III)
Eligibility: lost job or received notice, unlikely to return to current job or industry; long-term unemployed; self-employed, unemployed due to economic conditions or natural disaster; *Administration*: formula grants to State and local entities; *FY 1994 Appropriation*: $1,118.0 million.

Defense conversion assistance program (title III-B, Section 325)
Eligibility: same as "generic" program and laid off, terminated, or received notice as a result of reductions in defense spending or base closures; *Administration*: discretionary

grants to States, substate grantees, and others; *FY 1994 Appropriation:* no new funds appropriated for FY 1994. $150.0 million appropriated in FY 1991 is available for obligation through September 30, 1997.

Defense diversification program (title III-B, section 325 (a))
Eligibility: certain members of the armed forces, certain civilian employees of Department of Defense and Energy, and some defense contractor employees; *Administration:* discretionary grants to States, substate grantees, and others; *FY 1994 Appropriation:* no new funds appropriated for FY 1994. $75.0 million appropriated in FY 1993 is available for obligation through September 30, 1994.

Clean air employment transition assistance program (title III-B, section 326)
Eligibility: same as "generic " program and laid off, terminated, or received notice as a result of compliance with the Clean Air Act; *Administration:* discretionary grants to States, substate grantees, and others; *FY 1994 Appropriation:* no funds appropriated for FY 1994.

Native Americans programs (title IV-A, section 401)
Eligibility: Indians, Eskimos, Aleuts, Native Hawaiians, or other Native Americans; economically disadvantaged, unemployed, or underemployed; *Administration:* discretionary grants to tribal and other Native American groups; *FY 1994 Appropriation:* $64.2 million.

Migrant and seasonal farmworkers program (title IV-A, section 402)
Eligibility: migrant ad seasonal farmworkers and their dependents; *Administration:* discretionary grants to public, private, and nonprofit organizations; *FY 1994 Appropriation:* $85.6 million.

Job Corps (title IV-B)
Eligibility: age 14-24, economically disadvantaged; *Administration:* federally administered primarily through contracs with the corporations and nonprofit organizations; *FY 1994 Appropriation:* $1,040.5 million.

Veterans' employment programs (title IV-C)
Eligibility: service disable veterans, Vietnam veterans, and veterans recently separated from service; *Administration:* discretionary grants to States; *FY 1994 Appropriation:* $9.0 million.

Youth Fair Chance program (title IV-H)
Eligibility: age 14-30,; 16-19 for job guarantee program; *Administration:* discretionary grants to communities; *FY 1994 Appropriation:* $25.0 million.

Microenterprise grants program (title IV-H)
Eligibility: economically disadvantaged owners of commercial enterprise with five or fewer employees; *Administration:* discretionary grants to States and title IV-A grantees; *FY 1994 Appropriation:* $1.5 million.

Disaster relief employment assistance program (title IV-J)
Eligibility: eligible for JTPA dislocated workers program, Native American programs, or migrant and seasonal farmworker programs or unempoloyed as result of a disaster;

Administration: discretionary grants to States; *FY 1994 Appropriation*: no funds appropriated for FY 1994.

Jobs for Employable Dependent Individuals Incentive Bonus Program (title V)
Eligibility: States that have provided training to absent parents of children receiving Aid to Families with Dependent Children (AFDC) and /or blind or disabled recipients of Supplemental Security Income (SSI); *Administration*: bonus payments to States; *FY 1994 Appropriation*: no funds appropriated for FY 1994.

Discretionary grants are assistance awards in which Federal funds are allocated according to the determination of the administering Federal agency as to amounts and recipients. Formula grants are assistance awards in which Federal funds are allocated to States or their subdivisions according to a distribution formula prescribed by law or regulation.

Subject Index